The 5-Minute BIBLE STUDY for Men

Quentin Guy

The 5-Minute BIBLE STUDY for Men

Pursuing God

BARBOUR
PUBLISHING

Introduction

Can doing anything for just five minutes a day make a difference? Depends on how you spend it. Like a lot of life, your best-spent, most productive times come in short increments—the payoff for keeping your eye on the ball, so to speak. Clarity about what really matters comes in small bursts and often is the result of consistency. And what better way to learn about what matters most than to give God five solid minutes of your attention?

That's where this book comes in. Look at it as a key that helps you unlock the most important book of all: the Bible. When you give your Father in heaven even five good minutes every day, or as close to daily as possible, you'll see that He is the one who will get your attention.

Pursuing God is all about those moments of contact and connection. Your mission is simply to reach out to Him. He will meet you there, whether it's halfway or all the way. Each day's study centers on some aspect of what seeking God looks like—the challenges but also the peace and joy of knowing Him better.

So, how do you use those five minutes?

Minutes 1–2: **Read** carefully the scripture passage for each day's Bible study.

Minute 3: ***Understand***. Ponder a couple of prompts designed to help you apply the verses from the Bible. Consider these throughout your day.

Minute 4: ***Apply***. Read a reflection based on the day's scriptural focus. Think about what you are learning and how to apply these truths.

Minute 5: ***Pray***. A prayer starter will help you open a conversation with God. Remember to allow time for Him to speak into your life as well.

Reading *The 5-Minute Bible Study for Men: Pursuing God* means you're willing to take your shot at knowing God better, and that's fantastic—first, because He is worth the effort, but also because He really is right there, waiting with a full heart to hear from you. His Word is a game-changer. Carve out these five minutes every day—make it an appointment—and expect to see God make a difference in how you handle yourself, your day, and your relationships.

Who's Pursuing Whom?

Read John 6:41–45

KEY VERSE:

"No one can come to Me unless the Father who sent Me draws him [giving him the desire to come to Me]; and I will raise him up [from the dead] on the last day."

JOHN 6:44 AMP

UNDERSTAND:

- *What led you to commit your life to follow Christ?*
- *How was God working in your life leading up to that moment?*

APPLY:

We tend to pursue God the way we decide to start a hobby. We do the choosing—the activity, time, and place—and think we'll get better at being Christians if we just work at it. But before we can do anything for God, we need to understand we wouldn't even care about God if He didn't care about us first.

God is all-powerful, all-knowing, and everywhere present. He gave up what is most precious to Him so we might someday understand and respond to

His initiative. He enables our goodness and fixes our brokenness. With great acts of power, mercy, and love, He draws us to Himself.

Pursuing God starts by acknowledging He is the original pursuer. It's His overwhelming, all-in love we respond to when we say we're pursuing Him. As 1 John 4:19 (NKJV) notes, "We love Him because He first loved us."

The pursuit of God is comforting and challenging, calming and confounding. But that's God. He is both loving Father and holy Lord of all—closer than a brother and harder to grasp than quantum physics. God sacrificed His precious Son to save you, which imparts both terrible news (you're that much of a sinner) and good news (He thinks you're worth dying for).

PRAY:

Thank You, God, for thinking I'm worth pursuing. Help me to see all the times and ways You sought me out. I find comfort in knowing it's not up to me to find You because You found me first.

The Best Time

Read Psalm 63:1

KEY VERSE:

O God, You are my God; early will I seek You;
my soul thirsts for You; my flesh longs for You in
a dry and thirsty land where there is no water.
PSALM 63:1 NKJV

UNDERSTAND:

- *How has God refreshed you—by His Word, through a friend, a moment in nature? What did you learn about Him then?*

- *What time of day do you do your most creative and productive thinking and work?*

APPLY:

Hitting that Bible study first thing in the morning is certainly a great way to get your day rolling—if you can still remember what you studied by midmorning. But if you can't—if some aspect of your time with God is not sticking with you throughout the day—there's probably a better time for you to do it.

First, the hard question: Is your time with God just checking a box that makes you feel better about yourself? If it's no different a priority than a workout or taking the dog for a walk, then maybe it's time to rethink it.

Even if you're not at your sharpest in the morning, it's a great idea to start with a few words of thanks and praise. When it comes to focusing on learning about God and His Word, however, it's possible that there are better times than others.

In Psalm 63:1, David writes about seeking God early. However, *early* means more than first thing in the morning; it also means first, as a top priority. Whenever you seek God, be diligent and focused. Dedicate time to pursue Him when you're at your sharpest. Find your best time, and give God the first part of it.

PRAY:

Lord, I am truly grateful You are there whenever I make time for You. Help me find the best part of my day so I can give the first part of my best, most productive time to You.

Being Fully Known
Read Psalm 139:1–6

KEY VERSES:

O LORD, You have searched me and known me. You know my sitting down and my rising up; You understand my thought afar off.
PSALM 139:1–2 NKJV

UNDERSTAND:

- *God knows everything. How does that affect the way you approach relationships, decision-making, work?*

- *When was the last time you thought you knew better than God?*

APPLY:

God has perfect knowledge of every subject and topic the human mind can consider, plus far more that we can't. No one teaches God anything; He has nothing to learn and is never surprised. All the folks who think they will have questions for God when they see Him are in for a rude awakening. The superiority of His knowledge beggars the answers they think He owes them.

God knows everything about you. He knows the ways you're different on Sunday morning than Friday night. And He knows when your thoughts wander and where. You can protest what feels like an invasion of privacy, but He knows exactly what you're going to say.

We're contradictory creatures. We hate when people use information about us against us, yet we long to be known and understood by someone who is truly for us. When David wrote in Psalm 139:5 (NKJV), "You have hedged me behind and before, and laid Your hand upon me," he was squirming beneath the weight of God's omniscience, probably because he realized that all his comings and goings—every thought, word, and deed—weren't always pleasing to God.

God knows everything about you and still thinks you were worth dying for. He knows both who you are and who you are becoming in Christ—someone like Jesus, someone beyond your wildest dreams.

PRAY:

All-knowing God, I celebrate Your knowledge. You know my sin and my struggles, but You also know my salvation, sanctification, and success in Christ. I lay everything I know (and don't know) at Your feet. Help me know You better.

The Tense Comfort of God's Omnipresence

Read Psalm 139:7–12

Key Verse:

Even in darkness I cannot hide from you.
To you the night shines as bright as day.
Darkness and light are the same to you.
Psalm 139:12 nlt

Understand:

• *When was the last time you behaved as if God couldn't see you?*

• *When was the last time God comforted you in a hard moment?*

Apply:

God knows everything and is present in every place and moment. Does that comfort you or make you nervous? A little tension is good for any relationship —keeping us from taking the other person for granted—but especially with God. We cannot limit Him or fully understand Him.

In Psalm 139:6 (nlt), David described God's omniscience as "too great for me to understand." He realized there was nowhere he could go where God was not. He is equally and fully present in both light and darkness. We cannot escape accountability to God. The end of this life is the beginning of eternity.

Even for believers, that creates friction. Where is God in our suffering? We take comfort in a Romans 8:28 sense, knowing it's God's specialty to work good things out of bad, straight paths from crooked sticks. But we also know that God demands total control over our entire life. And man, is giving everything over to Him a process!

The Christian life is built on the belief that suffering has value and purpose in God's good hands. We are saved from hell but still challenged by our flesh, the world, and the devil. But even in our darkest hours, we are not hidden from Him. He is making all things right.

Pray:

Ever-present Lord, my humble thanks feel small and insufficient to express what You have done for me. Forgive me for the times I have resisted Your hand honing me into Jesus' image. Today I accept Your attention and trust Your purposes in all that happens.

The Real Wake-Up Call
Read Psalm 139:13–18

KEY VERSE:

When I awake, I am still with You.
PSALM 139:18 NKJV

UNDERSTAND:

- *How does God use His power on your behalf?*
- *When God says He won't ever leave or forsake you, how does that affect your daily life?*

APPLY:

God's unmatched power saturates your life from the moment of your conception through the moment of your death and into eternity. In Psalm 139:13–18, David praises the Lord's hand in creating his life in such an awe-inspiring fashion. God's great power works on the most personal level—the wonders of the cell, of pregnancy, of knowing exactly how long each of us will live. Then David tops it off: "When I awake, I am still with You." He was talking about more than a good night's rest.

Sleep is often a biblical metaphor for both physical and spiritual death. For the Christian, then, to wake up is to step into new life—salvation in this life and eternity with Christ after death. In some sense, David understood that death didn't have to be the final separation from God but a crossing of the threshold into eternal life with Him.

In Psalm 17:15 (NLT), David anticipated that moment: "Because I am righteous, I will see you. When I awake, I will see you face to face and be satisfied." We do the best we can and trust God to make sense of all the hard, broken things in this life. When we die, we will wake up to all that God has for us in eternity, knowing everything we need to know to be satisfied and fulfilled.

PRAY:

Father, I am amazed You use Your unbelievable, unlimited power to make a way in Christ so I can stand in Your presence. Wake me up to Your reality—who You are and what You are doing in, around, and through me. I can't wait to see You.

Costly Trust

Read Psalm 139:19–24

KEY VERSES:

Search me, O God, and know my heart; try me, and know my anxieties; and see if there is any wicked way in me, and lead me in the way everlasting.
PSALM 139:23–24 NKJV

UNDERSTAND:

- *What comes to mind when you think of God's holiness?*

- *What are the challenges of asking God to show how you can improve in living His way?*

APPLY:

God's most disquieting actions happen because He is holy: His judgment, wrath, justice, jealousy, and even vengeance. His other characteristics are much more comforting: His love, grace, mercy, and faithfulness.

And yet, holiness is the attribute of God mentioned most often in the Bible. In 1 Peter 1:16 (NKJV), He calls us to be holy: "Be holy, for I am holy." Holiness matters, but how do we practice it?

Like David in Psalm 139, we need to focus on a

right relationship with God. Christ makes that possible. In practice, holiness means we love what God loves and hate what He hates—not in a judgmental way, thinking ourselves superior, but understanding that sin has corrupted God's good creation and that we are desperate for Him to make things right.

He makes things right through Jesus. Christ in us makes us holy, set apart by God for God's purposes and pleasure. Our obedience demonstrates our desire to be holy like He is holy. As we do, we join with David who wrapped up Psalm 139:23 (NKJV) by opening himself up for divine scrutiny: "Search me, O God, and know my heart." Where David obeyed in anticipation, we obey in response to Jesus' finished work. When we do, we are His holiness in action.

PRAY:

Lord, I take comfort in knowing You are perfect in all of Your ways. I join my voice with the angels praising You, saying, "Holy, holy, holy, is the Lord God Almighty, who was and is and is to come" (Revelation 4:8 ESV).

Believing Is Seeing

Read Hebrews 11:1–6

KEY VERSE:

Without faith it is impossible to please him, for whoever would draw near to God must believe that he exists and that he rewards those who seek him.
HEBREWS 11:6 ESV

UNDERSTAND:

- *To the best of your recollection, list God's attributes and characteristics.*

- *What are the challenges of pursuing an invisible God?*

APPLY:

The pursuit of God is sometimes made more challenging by the fact that we can't see Him. It's so much easier to believe in what we can perceive with our senses, even though we know they are limited. But if faith was based only on what we could perceive, it would be science not faith. And even science has its limits.

God's interactions with us give faith an anchor in history. He made Himself known to people from the beginning and then made Himself visible in Jesus Christ. Even though we don't see the Holy Spirit enter us when we're saved, the proof of His presence is in the way He changes us. Hebrews 11:1 (NIV) says, "Faith is confidence in what we hope for and assurance about what we do not see." When we take that to heart, we don't stay the same. God teaches us to live in light of a greater world. Hebrews 11:16 (NIV) says we long for the reward of "a better country—a heavenly one."

Don't underestimate the anchoring power of that promised reward for the faithful. Believe that everything you go through now is worth it, that God sees you and will reward you for sticking with Him no matter what. Believing is seeing. Believe it now, when your flesh still clouds your eyes, and one day, you will see Him face-to-face.

PRAY:

Father, I get stuck in what my senses can perceive. Expand my view of You and all the ways, seen and unseen. Your invisibility reminds me that You are unlimited, greater than all my senses can perceive.

Word of Life

Read Psalm 119:1–11

Key Verses:

*Oh, that my actions would consistently reflect
your decrees! Then I will not be ashamed when
I compare my life with your commands.*
Psalm 119:5–6 NLT

Understand:

- *Do you read the Bible with a sense of anticipation
that God will tell you something about Himself or
your life that you need to hear?*

- *If not, will you commit to asking Him to show up
when you spend time in His Word?*

Apply:

Psalm 119 can be pretty intimidating to read and
absorb, partly because of its incredible length (it's
the longest chapter in the Bible), but also because
of its challenging theme: reliance on the Word of
God. Almost every verse (176 of them!) mentions
some reference to the scriptures—the law of the
Lord, His instructions, precepts, statutes, decrees,
and commandments.

The unnamed psalmist lays out the theme in Psalm 119:1–2 (NLT): "Joyful are people of integrity, who follow the instructions of the LORD. Joyful are those who obey his laws and search for him with all their hearts." Joy is different than happiness. Where happiness comes from fleeting circumstances, joy is a fruit of the Spirit (Galatians 5:22), an attitude that God deserves our deepest trust in everything we feel, think, and do.

Taking God's words into your heart is the only endeavor that guarantees a good outcome. Any other may fail—a business, a work of art, a relationship— but walking in God's ways brings (among other good things) freedom, joy, confidence, and comfort.

Even better, no earthly failure can define you. God redeems everything we give to Him, so that we can agree with Psalm 119:71 (NLT): "My suffering was good for me, for it taught me to pay attention to your decrees."

PRAY:

*Lord God, Your Word is life. Give me
a hunger to read it, know You more,
and live fruitfully as a result.*

Freedom Requires Sacrifice

Read 1 Kings 22:1–8, 26–28, 31–36

Key Verse:

Jehoshaphat said to the king of Israel,
"Inquire first for the word of the Lord."
1 Kings 22:5 ESV

Understand:

- *What does freedom look like to you?*

- *What's your tendency with God: to ask for permission or forgiveness?*

Apply:

Seeking what God has to say *before* you act is great advice, but in context there is a lot more to chew on.

First, look at the history: Jehoshaphat was one of the rare God-honoring kings in Israel and Judah's history, so before he allied himself with King Ahab of Israel, he wanted to see what God had to say to them. In those days, to hear from God, you asked a prophet.

Ahab knew that a true prophet would only have bad things to say to him. So he kept false prophets around: ear-ticklers and sycophants. But real freedom means accepting difficult-to-hear truths. "Inquiring first" of God means being open to His redirection, trusting He knows best.

Next, listen to the right message: Jehoshaphat knew of one prophet, Micaiah, who would speak God's truth no matter the cost to himself. And when Micaiah did, Ahab ordered him to be jailed until he himself returned from battle. Micaiah's response showed his trust in God: if God had spoken through him, Ahab would die in battle; if God hadn't, he wouldn't. It was a simple test he staked his freedom on.

Finally, live in touch with reality: Ahab attempted to disguise himself in battle, but he still died of a seemingly random arrow wound. Since God's will is going to happen whether you're on board or not, why not get on board? Prepare for whatever the day may bring by seeking God first. Offering your time to God with open hands and heart is a sacrifice, but one that pleases Him.

PRAY:

Lord God, today I commit myself to Your will. Open my eyes, ears, and heart to You. Show me what pleases You.

One in a Hundred

Read Matthew 18:11–14

Key Verse:

"If a man has a hundred sheep, and one of them goes astray, does he not leave the ninety-nine and go to the mountains to seek the one that is straying?"
Matthew 18:12 NKJV

Understand:

- *How do you react when you're driving and you realize you're lost? Do you keep going or seek directions?*

- *How quick are you to pray when things aren't going well?*

- *Do you realize you are special to God?*

Apply:

Getting spiritually lost looks similar to getting lost while driving. The Bible is your map, and the Holy Spirit is your divine GPS, but you still get off track. You thought you knew the way—how to pray, how to act humbly, how to lead yourself and your family—but then unfamiliar sights started showing up, followed by that nagging feeling that you're off course.

When the kids have gone haywire, communication

lines between you and your wife are down, and you're just not feeling like God is there, it's scary, and that fear can easily replace your confidence in God's sovereign care. So, you try to course-correct based on your own thoughts and get even more lost.

Whether you get physically lost driving or go spiritually astray, pride is often the biggest obstacle to getting back on track. God knows when you're lost. He also knows how to find you. Whatever may be keeping you from asking for help, your good Shepherd is still coming to find you. Stop trying to fix it/hide/act like you're okay. Stand still and call out. You may just be the one in a hundred He is looking for.

PRAY:

Father, I should've known better than to let things get this bad. Will You find me where I am and carry me back into Your light so I can see the right way to go again? Forgive my foolish pride and self-reliance—and thanks for always coming after me.

Getting Unstuck

Read Proverbs 8:17

KEY VERSE:

*I love those who love me; and those who
diligently seek me will find me.*
PROVERBS 8:17 NASB

UNDERSTAND:

- *What keeps you from spending as much time praying
  and reading the Bible as you think you should?*

- *What is your image of God as you spend time with
  Him? Impatient and frustrated or looking forward
  to it?*

APPLY:

God knows you're busy. While you're busy beating
yourself up because you can barely carve out five
minutes a day to focus on Him, He loves that you're
making time at all. After all, God can do more with
five minutes than you can with a whole week.

Don't get stuck thinking that God is tapping His
foot, arms folded, thinking you're a doofus because
you don't spend enough time building your faith and
too much time trying to fix things you can't control.

Instead, picture Him as your Father, waiting with open arms. He is there no matter what, willing and able to comfort, give wisdom, and show grace. He brings challenges sometimes, but everything He does is to help you learn, grow, and know Him better. If anything, He just wishes you would call Him more often, let Him know how you're doing, and thank Him for being a good dad.

If you're stuck in a rut and just need someone who understands that, Jesus does. He got worn out and beaten up too—but He allowed it so He could identify with you in your hard times and give you that deep understanding your soul is dying for. Focus on Him and let Him help you get unstuck.

PRAY:

Jesus, You went through the worst moments so I could turn to You when I'm in a bad spot. Thanks for being there for me. Will You keep being patient with me, waiting for me to call, and remind me how much You want to hear from me?

Quick to Forgive

Read Psalm 32

KEY VERSE:

*Finally, I confessed all my sins to you and
stopped trying to hide my guilt. I said to myself,
"I will confess my rebellion to the LORD."
And you forgave me! All my guilt is gone.*
PSALM 32:5 NLT

UNDERSTAND:

- *List specific things for which God has forgiven you.*

- *How hard is it for you to forgive others? Why?*

APPLY:

In Ephesians 4:32, Paul called us to forgive others
to the extent that Jesus has forgiven us. Why, then,
do we hang on to how we've been wronged or the
wrongs we've done? Accident or not, the damage is
real: sleeplessness results, nerves on edge, appetite
diminished—we carry the wrongdoing as a physical
weight, an emotional millstone. Surely God has more
for His children.

And so He does. But it all begins with forgiveness
—Him forgiving us. Our problems start when we

think we don't have much that needs to be forgiven or we're undeserving of what's happened. We're better than most, aren't we? But as Isaiah 64:6 (AMP) reminds us, "All our deeds of righteousness are like filthy rags."

Psalm 7:11 (NKJV) says, "God is a just judge, and God is angry with the wicked every day." Our offense is always against Him first and foremost—and yet, He longs to forgive us. Jesus obeyed the Father's will so we could be forgiven. Forgiveness isn't a matter of feeling but obedience. Especially under grace, we must forgive.

Loving what God loves is learning to forgive, especially when someone doesn't deserve it. When you do that, you will find yourself, as David did, surrounded by mercy. Let God's forgiveness wash over you anew.

PRAY:

Lord God, holy and just, forgive me for loving my filthy rags more than Your peace and security. When I value forgiveness like You do, I will be quicker to seek forgiveness and forgive others.

Trust Despite Confusion

Read Luke 2:41–52

KEY VERSE:

He said to them, "Why did you seek Me? Did you not know that I must be about My Father's business?"
LUKE 2:49 NKJV

UNDERSTAND:

- *What about God is hardest for you to understand?*

- *How difficult is it for you to trust God fully when you don't understand what He's doing?*

APPLY:

Imagine the thrill of horror that went through Joseph and Mary's hearts as they realized they had left Jesus behind in the enormous crowds leaving Jerusalem.

When they finally found Jesus, His response was just plain confusing. We've all heard bizarre and infuriatingly patronizing things come from the mouths of twelve-year-olds (if only because we remember being twelve!), but this is an all-timer: "You should've known I'd be hanging out in My (real) Father's house."

On one hand, Mary and Joseph might have been expecting an apology: "Sorry I scared you, Mom and

Dad." But then there is the whole reference to Jesus' Father, by which they knew He didn't mean Joseph, which brought up everything that was so alien to them about this boy they had raised and loved.

Sometimes what God's Word says isn't clear, and sometimes it is, but it cuts right to the core of an embarrassing habit. And yet, He knows best and cares the most, doesn't He?

Part of pursuing God is learning to deal with that tension. When Jesus confuses you, remember that He always wants His best for you, even when you can't see what He's doing. If you can trust Him at those key moments of uncertainty, fear, and desperate hope, He will not let you down.

PRAY:

Father, You're working things together in ways I can't begin to imagine. Help me reconcile what I don't know about what You're doing with what I do know about You. You are holy and just and running over with mercy, love, and grace. I trust You.

The Horizon of Recovery

Read Deuteronomy 4:26–31

KEY VERSE:

*If from there you seek the LORD your God,
you will find him if you seek him with all
your heart and with all your soul.*
DEUTERONOMY 4:29 NIV

UNDERSTAND:

• *What are some ways you seek God?*

• *How hard is it for you to turn back to God when
you've strayed away?*

APPLY:

Deuteronomy 4:29 (NIV) says, "If from there you
seek the LORD"—but where is *there*? At this point in
Israel's history, God had delivered the first generation
from Egypt after they'd blown it, constantly doubting
Him and turning back to their familiar idols. After
this latest fresh start, Moses predicted they would
blow it again. That's where the *there* comes in: from
that next point of sin and distress, they would call
out to God.

Fortunately, there was (and is) good news:

Deuteronomy 4:31 (NKJV) affirms that even when you blow it (again), God is right there, so that when you turn from your sin and back to Him and His ways, "He will not forsake you nor destroy you, nor forget the covenant of your fathers which He swore to them." God is always faithful to keep His promises, to do what is right. You just have to want it more than anything else.

The trajectory of seeking God has some huge ups and downs. But He is the steady line, the unchanging horizon that helps you reorient and look for Him again. When you make a habit of that—seeking Him and being willing to change based on what you learn—He will reward your faith by anchoring you to Himself.

PRAY:

Lord, You are unfailingly merciful and patient.
Thank You that You are making me more
and more sensitive to my sin, making me hate
it while loving You more and that You are
always right there when I turn back to You.

Spirit and Truth

Read John 4:23–26

Key Verses:

*"A time is coming, and even now has arrived,
when the true worshipers will worship the
Father in spirit and truth; for such people
the Father seeks to be His worshipers."*

John 4:23 NASB

Understand:

- *What is your favorite way to worship God?*

- *What distracts you from worshiping God with a
full, right heart?*

Apply:

Jesus makes an intriguing statement in John 4:24
in the middle of His discussion with the Samaritan
woman at the well: God is looking for those who
will worship Him "in spirit and truth." Their talk
had turned to worship. The Samaritans had Mount
Gerizim, their own local place where they worshiped
God, and the Jews had the temple in Jerusalem. This
woman wanted to know which was the right place,
but she was asking the wrong question.

The question isn't *where* but *whom*. That's what Jesus was getting at—to worship God in the way God approves is to consider twin factors: spirit and truth. There is only one who worships God in this committed, right-hearted way: Jesus Christ Himself. So, it is only because we are His that we can be a true worshipper.

In worship we should focus on what matters most to the Spirit—the glorification of Jesus Christ. Since Jesus Himself is the only true worshipper, our worship should focus on what means so much to Him: the good news of God's grace.

Anyone gathered in spirit and truth—disregarding barriers of class, gender, age, nationality, and ethnicity —is on track and ready to worship God the way He told us to: focused on God's will and words and celebrated among His people.

Pray:

God, You're great and deserving of all praise now and forever. I'm so grateful to be covered by the great gift of Jesus' love and sacrifice so I can be a true worshipper. Help me to worship You the way You said Your people should, in spirit and truth.

Nobody's Looking

Read Psalm 14

KEY VERSES:

The LORD looks down from heaven on the children of man, to see if there are any who understand, who seek after God. They have all turned aside; together they have become corrupt; there is none who does good, not even one.
PSALM 14:2–3 ESV

UNDERSTAND:

- *How do you tend to view nonbelievers—as knuckleheads or lost sheep?*

- *Which describes your general view of God better— wrathful judge or open-armed father?*

APPLY:

Some of us are really good at sharing about Jesus, but a lot of us hold back; we're introverts or don't want to be rejected or worried about blowing our reputation ("Yeah, he's a Christian, but don't worry—he's cool").

Psalm 14 is a wake-up call to stop caring about cool. The world is full of cool people who want nothing to do with God. Some of them hate God and anyone who wants anything to do with Him. Instead, tell them about Jesus.

We each have our stories about how God changed us through the gospel. Your story doesn't have to be spectacular; God's Spirit will make the impact because He knows each person's heart and how to reach everyone. Our part is sharing the gospel. Romans 10:17 (NIV) says, "Faith comes from hearing the message."

Trust the power of the message. Psalm 14:5–6 (ESV) says you are part of the "generation of the righteous," and the "LORD is [your] refuge." When you represent Him to this broken world, He has your back, no matter its reaction. Nobody is looking for Him, but we weren't either until we heard about Jesus.

PRAY:

I am so grateful, Father, for Your salvation in Jesus. I want to look for You and what You want to accomplish in this crazy world. Please inflate me with a sense of Your importance, the wonder and joy of what You have done and are doing, so I can't help but tell others about You.

The Mission

Read Hebrews 10:23–25

Key Verse:

Let us not neglect our meeting together, as some people do, but encourage one another, especially now that the day of his return is drawing near.
Hebrews 10:25 NLT

Understand:

- *What do you see as the value of church?*

- *How has God used other believers to help, build, and heal you?*

Apply:

God is all about relationship. The most harmonious, joyful relationship ever is shared among Father, Son, and Holy Spirit. So it makes sense that something special happens when God's people gather to worship Him and seek His face—that is, with no agenda other than to honor Him and deepen the relationship. Vital things happen in fellowship that can't happen when you're alone.

The church is Christ's body, all the parts working together to accomplish what He, as the head, wants.

At church, He wakes us up spiritually, reminding us both that we are separate from the world and of our shared mission to the world. The Spirit encourages us, builds us up, and heals us through worship and the teaching of the Word. God gets us out of our own heads and amplifies our joy because we're sharing it with others who are also relying on Him. These things can't happen anywhere else.

People have all kinds of reasons for attending church less often these days. Without invalidating some of those concerns, let's remember the benefits of church and not give up on gathering. We only have one life to be on mission with God. Let's take advantage of this precious season, lock shields with our brothers and sisters, and see what He does.

PRAY:

Lord God, You are worth more than anything this world can offer or threaten to take. You have provided with Your own blood a gathering place for Your people. Forgive me for when I haven't treated church as something essential and precious to You. Give me the hunger to join with Your people to seek Your face.

The Litmus Test for Trusting God

Read Luke 12:29–34

KEY VERSE:

*"Where your treasure is,
there your heart will be also."*
LUKE 12:34 NKJV

UNDERSTAND:

- *What is your process for making big decisions—marriage, parenting, jobs, houses, cars, and so on?*

- *What shows you more effectively how God loves you—His provision for what you need or for who you need to be?*

APPLY:

Getting vs. giving is the heart issue Jesus deals with in Luke 12, and His words dare us to address a very bottom-line subject: Who is God to us—a loving Father or a means to an end? You can't know what your answer really is until you've given yourself completely over to His priorities—giving because He gives, loving because He loves, serving because He serves.

What kind of God asks for that kind of trust? Only one who has given Himself, His very best, in Jesus Christ. Only one who has given up the worship of heaven for the hatred of men. Only one who chose to become poverty-stricken so you could become a king's heir. God's economy is upside-down in the world's eyes—putting yourself last to lift others up, giving to those who can't give back. But we do it because that's what He did.

Embrace Jesus and His counterintuitive ways and, rather than being driven by fear or greed or keeping up, you'll have clarity when financial difficulties arise or a tempting purchase looms. You'll see your investment in the kingdom is worth more than anything the world can offer—and best of all, unlike wealth or material things, your rewards await you in eternity.

PRAY:

Heavenly Father, You are the ultimate provider. You met my greatest need—forgiveness—in Christ; but with You, that's just the beginning of all You have for me. Free me from worry's unending grind by keeping Yourself in Your rightful place on the throne of my heart.

Wrestling with God

Read Genesis 32:24–26

KEY VERSE:

He said, "Let Me go, for the day breaks." But [Jacob] said, "I will not let You go unless You bless me!"
GENESIS 32:26 NKJV

UNDERSTAND:

- *When has God used something hard to draw you closer to Him?*

- *How relentless are you in seeking God's blessing?*

APPLY:

Jacob was a religious dude from a religious family. All his life, he had heard about his dad and grandfather's encounters with God—the miraculous deliverances, the life-changing tests of faith, the blessings of provision and purpose. And yet, from the moment of his birth, Jacob's behavior was characterized by sneakiness, lies, and thievery.

God wasn't real to him. While Jacob had no reason to doubt the stories his dad and grandpa told, for him, that's all they were—stories. Jacob did what was required to honor God, at least superficially, and that was enough for him. But that wasn't enough for God.

God literally got in his face and grappled with him because He knew that's what it would take to break through Jacob's self-reliance—and boy did He break through! Once Jacob realized who he was battling, he wouldn't let go until God blessed him, but he didn't walk away unscathed. God touched Jacob's hip and *pop!* Game over. Jacob walked with a limp for the rest of his life.

Hardship and hard questions remind you that God exists and that He wants you to seek Him. Let Him cut away everything keeping you from really knowing Him, even if what He prunes seems like a good thing. If you trust Him no matter what, you've moved from religion to relationship. Don't let go until He blesses you.

PRAY:

Almighty God, You made me with a purpose, and You reserve the right to break me for the same purpose—to know You more. Let me see Your face in the hard times, and strengthen me to endure in expectation of Your blessing.

God Loves an Underdog

Read 2 Corinthians 5:14–19

KEY VERSES:

If anyone is in Christ, he is a new creation. The old has passed away; behold, the new has come. All this is from God, who through Christ reconciled us to himself and gave us the ministry of reconciliation.
2 CORINTHIANS 5:17–18 ESV

UNDERSTAND:

- *Do you prefer underdogs or favorites?*

- *What do you think it means to let the love of Christ control you?*

APPLY:

We know God loves an underdog—just look at David, chosen because, as 1 Samuel 16:7 (MSG) declares, "GOD judges persons differently than humans do. Men and women look at the face; GOD looks into the heart."

David's whole story, though, reveals the trap we often fall into as Christians: we come to faith because we see ourselves properly in relation to God, as massive underdogs. Then we get comfortable being on the winning side and start to view ourselves as favorites, like the job's done. That's where David got into trouble; he got comfortable and took his favored status with God for granted.

To live life well, we need a growing relationship with Jesus. We must make a priority of what matters most to Him—seeking the highest good of as many others as we can so we can help populate His kingdom. As Paul noted in 2 Corinthians 5:14 (ESV), "The love of Christ controls us."

Jesus died for everyone so that as many as possible can live for Him. Since God doesn't see us the way the world does, we can't look at anyone else the way the world does—no quick judgments, no assuming the worst, only the effort to see others through God's eyes of love and grace.

PRAY:

I praise You, Lord, for saving me—for becoming human, setting Yourself up as the greatest underdog ever. Increase my compassion for the lost by reminding me of how You rescued me when I was lost.

No Holding Back

Read Psalm 37:1–6

Key Verse:

Delight yourself in the Lord; and He will give you the desires of your heart.
Psalm 37:4 NASB

Understand:

- *What do you think it means to delight in the Lord?*

- *Do you ever catch yourself holding something back from God—a habit, thought, or decision? If so, what's your response?*

Apply:

The movie *Gattaca* is the story of two brothers, one genetically perfected in the womb (Anton), the other (Vincent) left to his own inferior natural devices. As boys, they test each other by swimming out into the ocean as far as they dare in a game of chicken Anton always won. As adults, they engage in one final swim, and Anton almost drowns. Vincent, his substandard brother, saves him. When Anton asks how he pulled it off, Vincent replies, "I never saved anything for the swim back."

A model of manhood has always been marked by self-sufficiency, by the will to do what is necessary to succeed, sometimes at any cost. A so-called real man puts his stamp on the world, even if other, weaker people end up getting stamped along the way. Those are the men who David referred to in Psalm 37 as evildoers and fools because they rejected God in favor of self-sufficiency.

If your goals center on honoring God in all you do, you can run your race with boldness and confidence. Keep pushing to love well, to honor God, because you know He is with you. When Jesus came, that was God saving nothing for the swim back. He matches you stroke for stroke and keeps your head above water when you need Him most. Delight in Him because He delights in you—and keep swimming.

PRAY:

I need You today, Jesus. The race is long and hard, and I'm worn out. Remind me that You are with me and for me. Renew my delight in You and Your ways. Strengthen my trust in Your presence and provision. Help me to swim without fear.

Higher Ways,
Higher Thoughts

Read Isaiah 55:6–11

KEY VERSES:

*"For my thoughts are not your thoughts,
neither are your ways my ways," declares the
LORD. "As the heavens are higher than the
earth, so are my ways higher than your ways
and my thoughts than your thoughts."*
ISAIAH 55:8–9 NIV

UNDERSTAND:

- *Think of a time when God seemed to let you down.
How did you get back on track with Him?*

- *What is the difference between certainty in what
God does versus trust in who God is?*

APPLY:

Only a dishonest Christian says he has never been
disappointed with God's response to a prayer. There
is an ebb and flow to walking with God, times
when He feels wonderfully near and others when
He seems nowhere to be found. When you're in the
groove with God, nothing's better. Why can't it be

like that all the time?

The Bible makes it clear that God is always near. We're the ones who move away from Him. Maybe He allows it for a season and a purpose, the way He did in Genesis 40, when Joseph was seemingly forgotten in jail. Or maybe we've slipped and He's course-correcting us.

When we believe we have God figured out and then He does something we don't understand, it's easy to become bitter. Some even leave the faith because they think God's view of people is less loving, less righteous, and less merciful than theirs. But we cannot forget who God is, that even in our confusion and frustration, He never wastes our pain and He never forsakes us.

No matter how far you have drifted from Him, turn to Him without hesitation or reservation. Isaiah 55:7 (NLT) says God "will forgive generously." He just wants you back on board.

PRAY:

Lord, today I trust in who You are and who I am to You. Forgive me for thinking I've got You completely figured out. Your ways and thoughts are higher than mine. Bring me back into Your presence. I need You.

On the Straight and Narrow

Read Luke 13:24–27

KEY VERSE:

"Strive to enter through the narrow gate, for many, I say to you, will seek to enter and will not be able."
LUKE 13:24 NKJV

UNDERSTAND:

- *What parts of worldly thinking and living do you find most attractive?*

- *In what area of your life is it hardest to submit to God?*

APPLY:

What difference does it make whether we believe in God or not? Do the details of our spirituality really matter? Wouldn't it be easier to just let folks live the best lives they could?

At first, yes, much easier. However, that way of thinking and living is what Jesus called the wide gate "that leads to destruction" (Matthew 7:13 NIV). If all those good people were being honest, they would probably agree that, for all their virtuous behavior, life's meaning is still confusing, and going with the flow is ultimately empty. But they still dismiss God as a solution. Ultimately, God will honor their free will by giving them an eternity without Him.

But what do we do with Luke 13:27 (NKJV), where we see people who call themselves Christians being rejected by Jesus as "workers of iniquity"? Luke 13 points to the heart of the problem—the appearance of righteousness versus actual righteousness.

God alone knows the difference because He alone is actually righteous. That's why the gate that leads to life is narrow—the width of a Man hanging on a crucifix. Only Jesus walked a straight and true path—the one He paved for any who would follow Him. We can't love God without loving His rescue plan, without loving others and wanting to see them get through that skinny gate.

PRAY:

You alone are deserving of praise and glory, Almighty God. You alone are good, and You alone are worthy of my trust. You alone can save me. Lead me on the narrow path for Your glory and my best life.

The Root of Fear

Read Psalm 34:1–9, 1 Samuel 21:10–15

KEY VERSE:

I sought the LORD and He answered me,
and rescued me from all my fears.
PSALM 34:4 NASB

UNDERSTAND:

- *What frightens you the most?*

- *When was the last time you worried about people's opinions more than God's?*

APPLY:

David wrote Psalm 34 when Saul tried to kill him. Saul was jealous that God had chosen someone else to be king. Both men were reacting to frightening situations, but the contrast between their responses is telling.

David faced trouble by relying on God, but Saul chose his own devices, which separated him more and more from God. David feared God more than men; it was the opposite for Saul. David cared more about what God thought of him than his reputation or standing before people, even though it meant going on the run; Saul chose expedience at every turn. In the end, only David had the strength to stand.

For so many men, fear is one of their strongest motivators. We're afraid of failure, often of intimacy, of being revealed to be a fraud (especially when we've been successful). We avoid situations where we might not succeed because we're afraid our failures would define us. We don't let people get to know us because they might reject us. We don't dare admit we don't know how to do something at work because our boss might think it was a bad move to promote us. But God has more for us than that.

David admitted he was afraid and gave the situation to God, who helped him get through it and ultimately vindicated him. When you hold nothing back from God, fear loses its grip and faith takes hold.

PRAY:

Father, I confess I'm slow to admit what frightens me. I want to live boldly, trusting in Your love, strength, and provision. Help me to work hard at what I can control and leave the rest to You.

Hard Words to Stomach

Read John 6:33–40

KEY VERSES:

Jesus said to them, "I am the bread of life. He who comes to Me shall never hunger, and he who believes in Me shall never thirst. But I said to you that you have seen Me and yet do not believe."
JOHN 6:35–36 NKJV

UNDERSTAND:

- *How do you view tension—as a necessary source of growth or something to be avoided as a show of faith?*

- *Why is Jesus a leader worth following?*

APPLY:

Kingdom values look upside down compared to the ways and means of the world. From a human perspective, it doesn't make much sense to put yourself last so you can be first. Letting God vindicate you when you've been wronged requires ridiculous patience. Forgiving people—taking the burden of their wrongdoing on your shoulders—when they don't even acknowledge they've wronged you just isn't natural.

But everything Jesus asks you to do, He has done first. He gave up the eternal, loving community of the Trinity and the praise of heaven to draw us into relationship. He endured the most unjust punishment in history, choosing at Gethsemane to give God the final word on the third day. Even on the cross, He asked His Father to forgive His killers.

You may feel crushed, abandoned, and weak, but because of God's power in you, you are not. You are strong enough because He is. The supernatural is in you today and every day. Don't diminish its small movements or less flashy manifestations—faithful prayer, hopeful expectation, spiritual fruit. All of that is where you'll connect with God's heart, and that's the greatest miracle of all.

PRAY:

Lord God, You can do anything and everything that aligns with who You are and what You want. Because Your power is in me, I can follow Your example in trusting God and loving others. Open my eyes to see You at work all around me in big and small ways.

Let It Rip, Then Lift Him Up

Read Lamentations 5:15–22

KEY VERSE:

Restore us, O LORD, and bring us back to you
again! Give us back the joys we once had!
LAMENTATIONS 5:21 NLT

UNDERSTAND:

- *What do you tend to do when God seems far away?*

- *How often do you get angry, and what happens*
  when you do? Do you clam up or blow up (or clam
  up until you blow up)?

APPLY:

As we look at our wounded world, Jeremiah's lament
is a good model for us. He was honest about the
hurt and anger he felt, but mostly he identified with
his people, using *us* as he asked God why He had
abandoned and rejected His people.

When we cry out to God, He can handle it. He
isn't obligated to do what we ask, but He can understand why we're angry, sad, and fed up. Sin angers
Him all the time—but love is His very nature. Even
when God punishes His people, He does so with

higher purposes in mind—restoration, reconciliation, redemption.

Go ahead and get angry that the world's gone mad. Then remember David's words in Psalm 4:4 (NKJV): "Be angry, and do not sin." Let God channel your anger into a focus on obedience and justice, on pursuing right standing with Him and those around you. You're a new creation, after all. You're no longer bound by the idea that good Christians don't get mad. Don't go nuts, but don't clam up till you blow up. Instead, stand on Christ's righteous foundation, take on His mission, and do something about the problems you see.

PRAY:

God, You are the only one who is good, righteous, just, and loving. Please help me to see people through Your eyes and with Your heart. We are broken and riddled with sin and its consequences but still beloved and precious to You. Forgive me, forgive my country, forgive us all, merciful God, and bring our hearts into unity with Yours. Start with me.

Just Keep Plowing

Read Hosea 10:12–13

KEY VERSE:

"Plant the good seeds of righteousness, and you will harvest a crop of love. Plow up the hard ground of your hearts, for now is the time to seek the LORD, that he may come and shower righteousness upon you."
HOSEA 10:12 NLT

UNDERSTAND:

- *How regularly do you rely on God's righteousness to give you faith in hard times?*

- *How often do you think of your role as God's ambassador in the world?*

APPLY:

Hosea is one of those no-holds-barred OT prophets who made it clear that if even God's people reject Him long enough, He will let them have what they want. Case in point, the Babylonian exile—one of the lowest points in Israel's history. Hosea 10:13 (NKJV) describes the root of all Israel's sins: "You have eaten the fruit of lies, because you trusted in your own way."

Only God can insert a ray of hope into a message of dire judgment and mean it. But the fact that He does should inspire us to keep hope's flame burning in a darkening world. Even as Israel's doom was laid out, Hosea passed along a message of hope, Hosea 10:12's promise of God's faithfulness at all times. When we seek God's righteousness, He is faithful to bless us with all we need to do His work.

That's the only hopeful verse in a chapter of violent darkness, but it reminds us that no matter how overwhelmingly bad things get, God's light is never completely extinguished. Your part is to keep plowing the fields, to keep sowing His good news, especially when the light seems dimmest. Remind yourself and others that as bad as things get, God has provided a harvest—hope now and life forever.

PRAY:

Lord God, You remain faithful in every age. You are just in Your judgments, and Your mercies are truly astounding. These are troubled times, and I admit I'm often overwhelmed. Remind me today of the times You have rekindled my hope, and use me to reignite Your flame in other's hearts.

How to Use Your Freedom

Read 1 Corinthians 10:23–24

KEY VERSES:

All things are permitted, but not all things are of benefit. All things are permitted, but not all things build people up. No one is to seek his own advantage, but rather that of his neighbor.
1 CORINTHIANS 10:23–24 NASB

UNDERSTAND:

- *What has Christ set you free from, both generally and personally?*

- *When is it hardest to put others' needs ahead of your own? What makes it difficult?*

APPLY:

John 8:36 (NLT) shows us that an effective witness begins with the liberation Christ purchased for us: "If the Son sets you free, you are truly free." Being set free from sin is all-encompassing: we are new creations in Christ, raised with Him from the dead spiritual state we were born into. Not only do we have His power in us to stop our bad habits, but we are also free from fitting into the world's mold.

That freedom, however, carries responsibility. God's grace reminds us to treat others the way He treats us, with respect for our free will and a relentless desire for our highest good. His Spirit in us inspires and strengthens us to obey out of love, from the same position of humility Jesus assumed with us.

After all, Jesus needed nothing when He came from heaven to rescue us. He did so because He wanted to please the Father and build a bridge to reunite God with His creation.

Stay mindful of how your choices in nonessential matters impact other believers. Err on the side of caution out of love, and as Paul said in 1 Corinthians 10:31 (NASB), "Whatever you do, do all things for the glory of God."

PRAY:

Lord Jesus, the incredible cost You paid reminds me that true freedom isn't free, that it involves sacrificial love. Help me find the rhythm of enjoying the freedom You give me and respect the choices others make as they also seek to honor You.

Waiting on Justice, Living Out Mercy

Read Psalm 9:1–10

KEY VERSE:

Those who know Your name [who have experienced Your precious mercy] will put their confident trust in You, for You, O LORD, have not abandoned those who seek You.
PSALM 9:10 AMP

UNDERSTAND:

- *How do you tend to see God's general attitude toward people, as one of wrath or grace?*

- *How does your view of God impact your heart toward people?*

APPLY:

Compassion fatigue is real, and it can limit our desire for justice. The world is such a mess that it's easier not to care. The alternative—getting too deep in the weeds of daily headlines and the trials and problems of others—is no better. But there is more for the Christian than a seesaw between apathy and anger, and it starts with God.

Psalm 9 reminds us that God is paying attention to current events, as He has throughout history. He isn't blowing stuff off, and His temper isn't like ours—a cartoon thermometer boiling into the red with explosive fury. His anger at sin is righteous and just—and yet, He is always good, just, and loving. He also has knowledge and perspective we don't, and our only real decision is whether we're going to trust Him to do what's right.

God will "judge the world in righteousness" but He is also "a refuge and a stronghold for the oppressed" (Psalm 9:8–9 AMP). He perfectly strikes the proper balance of truth and love at all times and in all situations. Neither the times you've been wronged nor the times you've wronged others escape His notice. And whenever He chooses to deal with those injustices is the right time, whether in this life or the next.

PRAY:

Almighty God, Your mercies are overwhelming and Your grace is amazing. Your love demands both justice and mercy. Help me to be Your agent for both today in whatever situations You set before me.

Getting to the Heart of What Matters

Read Galatians 1:10–12

KEY VERSE:

Am I now trying to win the favor and approval of men, or of God? Or am I seeking to please someone? If I were still trying to be popular with men, I would not be a bond-servant of Christ.
GALATIANS 1:10 AMP

UNDERSTAND:

- *What does putting God first look like?*

- *When have you put your desire to please people over your desire to please God?*

APPLY:

Tests are God's way of making sure you understand that following Christ was never meant to be comfortable or undertaken without consideration for what it will cost you. Just as it cost God everything to save you, you must decide what you will give up to follow Him.

At the heart of every test is the issue of surrender. What is God asking you to surrender to Him?

Questions of evil and injustice? Bitterness over the hypocrisy you see in your church? Is it the feeling of God's absence at a critical moment?

When Paul says, "If I were still trying to be popular with men, I would not be a bond-servant of Christ," it's clear that the heart of his conversion hinged on sorting out what mattered most to him. He was basically the same man, but his view of God changed. He reordered his priorities, putting God first instead of his own accomplishments, views, background, or questions.

Because Paul saw God differently, he saw himself differently, and he learned to see others with fresh eyes. When what matters most to God matters most to you, your heart will change, and so will your corner of the world.

PRAY:

Lord Jesus, forgive me for the times I give more weight to other people's opinions than Yours. Show me anything about myself—any habits or ways of thinking about You or myself or others—that keeps me from putting You first in everything I am and do.

Taming the
Green-Eyed Monster

Read Deuteronomy 4:23–24

KEY VERSE:

*"The Lord your God is a consuming
fire, a jealous God."*
DEUTERONOMY 4:24 NASB

UNDERSTAND:

- *What is worth fighting for?*

- *What makes you jealous?*

- *What do you think of when God says He is jealous?*

APPLY:

We get nervous when we read that God is jealous.
It's one of mankind's worst traits, so how could it
possibly be any part of God's character? But dozens
of verses speak of Him this way.

Here's the difference: God is jealous for His
good name and for His people's hearts. He is jealous
because He is holy, loving what He loves and hating
what He hates with a purity of purpose and passion
we cannot imagine.

Human jealousy is driven by envy—the selfish

lust for what someone else has because we want to be superior in things like material goods, relationships, or reputation. Sin warps our desire to love and be loved by someone else completely into envy.

How, then, do we identify and fight our jealousy? As 1 Corinthians 6:19–20 (NIV) says, if you call Jesus Lord and Savior, you are "not your own; you were bought at a price." Jesus thus reserves the right to burn away everything that keeps you from being fully unified with Him. Christ's sacrifice consumes all your old ways, including your envy.

God wants us to want Him more than anything or anyone else. When we do, His Spirit in us purifies our desires and intentions. Over time, we learn to distinguish between our harmful, futile envy and His relentless, jealous love. With His help, we practice putting others' needs ahead of our own, wanting God's best for them more than anything else.

PRAY:

Forgive me, Father, for the times and ways I've been jealous. I turn my sin over to You to be burned away in Your consuming fire. If anything remains, I know it will be for the benefit of others and Your glory.

God Has Your Back

Read Hebrews 2:14–18

KEY VERSE:

Because he himself suffered when he was tempted,
he is able to help those who are being tempted.
HEBREWS 2:18 NIV

UNDERSTAND:

- *What temptations most often befall you? What keeps*
  you from asking God for help?

- *What is your expectation when you ask God to help*
  you overcome temptation?

APPLY:

To be human is to be tempted—even Jesus was
tempted by Satan, which tells us that temptation
itself isn't a sin. Our response is what matters. We
forget who God is and what He has done to help
us overcome our struggles with our flesh, the world,
and the devil.

God limits the strength of temptation so you can
bear it, and He gives you a way out (1 Corinthians
10:13). Even so, expect a struggle. Jesus died to set
you free, but He suffered to do it. Jesus didn't want

the cup of God's wrath, but He knew God would provide the way through and that the reward (which includes you) would be worth the pain.

Jesus knows what it's like to stare down temptation. Hebrews 4:15–16 (NLT) assures us "he faced all of the same testings we do, yet he did not sin. So let us come boldly to the throne of our gracious God. There we will receive his mercy, and we will find grace to help us when we need it most."

Come boldly means to cry out to God with the expectation that no matter how strong the impulse is, He will help you fight and overcome it. Pray, fast, read scripture, and keep seeking His face till the terrible moment passes. Like Jesus, you will have to suffer to conquer temptation—but you can.

PRAY:

Lord Jesus, You know what it's like to be tempted to choose the easier path, to choose immediate gratification over holiness, but You chose the Father's will when it counted the most. Give me Your power to withstand temptation at each moment of truth.

Take Time to Remember

Read Psalm 105:1–11

KEY VERSE:

*Search for the LORD and for his
strength; continually seek him.*
PSALM 105:4 NLT

UNDERSTAND:

- *You're a part of God's astonishing history with all mankind. How does that make you feel?*

- *When is the last time God did something significant in your life? How did you celebrate that?*

APPLY:

Psalm 105 praises God by looking back at the first part of His history with Israel. We see the pattern God established at creation that continues through this very day in the Church age: taking barren hearts and making something fruitful. God looked at formless chaos and spoke the world and everything in it into existence.

Then He built a nation out of an unlikely bunch of wanderers and called it His own, putting Israel at the center of redemptive history. Jesus chose to be born into poverty and assembled a motley crew to spread His good news, changing the world. That's where you come in. You are part of God's story, through His grace and love a saint and coheir with Christ, and He has important things for you to do.

Throughout God's dealings with us is the command to remember. When God-centered things happened to saints of old, they built monuments. They celebrated God's triumph, whether by building piles of stones, celebrating high holy days, or recalling God's deeds in worship.

What are the monuments marking your history with God? Part of pursuing God is recalling His faithfulness. Find ways to remind yourself to thank and praise Him. Whatever you do, remember Him on those dates.

PRAY:

Thank You, Lord, that You have made me a part of Your story. Your love, care, and provision are evidence of how great You are. Forgive me for the times when I forget all You have done and all You are doing now. Let my life be a monument to Your love.

Grace upon Grace

Read John 1:14–16

KEY VERSE:

For out of His fullness [the superabundance of His grace and truth] we have all received grace upon grace [spiritual blessing upon spiritual blessing, favor upon favor, and gift heaped upon gift].
JOHN 1:16 AMP

UNDERSTAND:

- *How does God's love affect your behavior on a daily basis?*

- *How hard is it for you to accept things you haven't earned?*

APPLY:

The wonder of Jesus' exchange on the cross is He got all the bad stuff our sinful natures and behavior deserve, while we receive everything He deserves. As Ephesians 2:8–9 says, salvation is an undeserved, unexpected gift given by grace.

But God's favor doesn't stop when you receive Christ; it's only beginning. Once you are under the power of grace instead of sin, you should expect a constant outpouring of what John called His "fullness." As James 4:6 (ESV) puts it, throughout our time with Jesus, "He gives more grace." Grace includes God seeing us through the lens of Jesus' righteousness.

If God pouring out grace upon grace on you makes you feel unworthy, remember that's how grace works. God sees what you're becoming and what you will become—the image of Christ. Let God bless you, cover you, favor you, and be delighted with you—because He wants you to share the overflow of His grace with others.

Imagine a heart so full of His grace that you bless your enemies, that you speak God's redeeming truth to someone who has spoken lies about you. You are His beloved son, and He is pleased with you. Let that truth encourage you to see others through that grace-filled lens.

PRAY:

Lord Jesus, Your grace overwhelms me. I don't deserve it, but I need Your help to move past that attitude of unworthiness into a habit of grace. You saved me so You could love me relentlessly and lavishly and so I could be a conduit of that love and grace to others.

No More Cat-and-Mouse

Read Luke 11:1–13

KEY VERSE:

"Don't bargain with God. Be direct. Ask for what you need. This is not a cat-and-mouse, hide-and-seek game we're in."
LUKE 11:10 MSG

UNDERSTAND:

- *How hard is prayer for you? What makes it difficult?*

- *What do you think God's best for you is?*

APPLY:

Prayer is challenging because it reminds us of our reliance on God. When things are going well, it's human nature to leave prayer for mealtimes, because hey, things are going well. When things are not going well, we often complain first, try to place blame somewhere, or work on fixing the issue—leaving prayer as a last resort: "Well, I guess the only thing we can do now is pray."

When we fail to pray as a first option—to avail ourselves of our Christ-bought access to God—we default to self-sufficiency. And then we blame God when we're not enough. That suggests we aren't really trusting God—at least not more than we trust ourselves. We treat God like a good backup plan.

We end up trying to game God with our prayers—to make sure we're using the right-sounding words, to pester Him like creditors seeking payment. We fear an answer of *wait* or *no*, as if a *yes* means God is finally seeing things the way we think they should be.

But when Jesus taught His followers to pray, He encouraged the boldness and persistence that comes from a healthy relationship. We are sons, and God is our Father. Do we love Him for who He is or what He can do for us? Either way, our prayer life reflects that basic attitude.

Pray:

Jesus, teach me to pray the way You pray. Let Your way become my way. Like a son coming to a beloved Father, I will be humble and bold, hopeful and persistent, trusting You know what's best.

Worship on Manual

Read 1 Chronicles 16:1–4, 8–12, 34–36

Key Verse:

Boast in His holy name; let the heart of those who seek the Lord be joyful.
1 Chronicles 16:10 NASB

Understand:

- *Aside from church services, when do you usually make time to worship God?*

- *Do you ever find yourself worshiping on autopilot?*

Apply:

In 1 Chronicles 16, David brought the ark to Jerusalem for the first time, placed it in the tabernacle as the focal point of God's presence, and led a God-honoring celebration, ending with the people shouting *amen* and praising the Lord. God was front and center, and all hearts were focused on Him.

If only every time we gathered for worship could be like that! Too often, we get stuck on music style or song length, or we just get bored and go through the motions. Regardless of our feelings, we should always bear in mind that, as John 4:24 (NKJV) says,

God is looking for those who worship Him in "spirit and truth."

Even David didn't just automatically get it right—in fact, he had messed up royally not too long before this glorious moment, when Israel didn't follow God's specific instructions about bringing the ark back to Jerusalem and someone died.

First Chronicles 16 shows us that David did it right the second time. The hard lesson he learned is that God reserves the right to tell us how He wants to be worshiped. The next time you're feeling itchy about worship, engage your heart first. Are you seeking to worship Him His way? God deserves all your attention.

Pray:

Father God, I want to worship You in spirit and truth. Forgive me for the times I've gotten stuck on a nonessential issue, and help me to keep my eyes on You, Your truth as expressed in Your Word, and Your heart as expressed in Jesus Christ. You deserve my full attention.

The Deepest Cut

Read Romans 2:25–29

KEY VERSE:

*True circumcision is not merely obeying the letter
of the law; rather, it is a change of heart produced
by the Spirit. And a person with a changed
heart seeks praise from God, not from people.*
ROMANS 2:29 NLT

UNDERSTAND:

- *What makes you want to obey God?*

- *How challenging is it for you to let the Holy Spirit
do His work in you rather than trying to do His
job yourself?*

APPLY:

When God made His covenant with Abraham, circumcision was a serious part of the covenant: to go uncircumcised was to be cut off from the covenant, from God, and His chosen people. This continued as a requirement in the Law of Moses.

Christians are not required to be circumcised simply because, as Galatians 2:16 (NKJV) says, "By the works of the law no flesh shall be justified."

God wants a deeper cut—one that goes straight to the heart, that does away with all the excuses, the secret agendas, the sense of superiority we get when we obey His commands. In Romans 2, Paul makes it clear that such a wound only comes from receiving Christ's saving work as a free gift. Jesus was wounded on our behalf so we would never have to be cut off from God.

True circumcision depends on the work of the Spirit in us. He creates the change of heart that wants what pleases God more than anything else. Our part is to learn what He wants, then let Him do His work in us. Don't let anything get in the way of that.

Pray:

Lord God, forgive me for the times I've let rule-keeping and the appearance of holiness keep me from loving You wholeheartedly. I acknowledge that I haven't loved You or others like You want me to. Help me obey You out of love and not performance.

Are You Coachable?

Read 2 Timothy 3:10–17

KEY VERSES:

All Scripture is inspired by God and is useful to teach us what is true and to make us realize what is wrong in our lives. It corrects us when we are wrong and teaches us to do what is right. God uses it to prepare and equip his people to do every good work.
2 TIMOTHY 3:16–17 NLT

UNDERSTAND:

- *When was the last time you trusted God and acted based on something you read in the Bible?*

- *Based on your decision-making process, how much of your confidence is in God and how much is in yourself?*

APPLY:

Thankfully, God's wisdom doesn't depend on our age or experience, but rather on our experience of Him. God is faithful to provide wake-up calls—to remind us He wants all of us at all times.

Those wake-up calls can be subtle redirections of the way we're thinking about something, or they can be devastating breakdowns of life as we knew it. However, they are all tests—to see if we truly put our faith in God and if we're committed to doing what the Bible teaches us.

God's Word is more than just a book. Its deeper truth changes lives. We pursue not a place but a Person—not blessings or heaven but Jesus Himself. But we need His help—and that's why He gave us the ultimate coach, His Spirit, and the ultimate playbook, the Bible.

Be coachable. Let God's patience inspire you to be humble when God redirects you. Remember, He is equipping you for every good work.

PRAY:

Father, please show me the areas of my life that You want to work on. I know this is a dangerous prayer, but I also know You are faithful and that all You do is for my good and Your glory. Give me the wisdom I need to see areas of improvement and work on them.

The Mirror Doesn't Lie

Read James 4:1–10

KEY VERSE:

Come close to God, and God will come close to you.
Wash your hands, you sinners; purify your hearts, for
your loyalty is divided between God and the world.
JAMES 4:8 NLT

UNDERSTAND:

- *How has God shown His love and loyalty to you?*

- *What makes it hard for you to offer those virtues in*
  return to Him?

APPLY:

James is great because he is so blunt and practical.
You don't go to James for a spiritual hug, but for an
unblinking look at how you're living out your faith.
You read James expecting a little course correction—
and he doesn't disappoint.

Look at his verbs in James 4:7–10 NKJV: *submit,*
resist, draw near, cleanse, purify, lament and *mourn*
and *weep, humble yourself.* These are strong verbs,
demanding wholehearted action. It's no surprise,
coming from the guy who told us to view trouble

as an opportunity for joy (James 1:2), who warned us that our own ungodly desires eventually conceive and deliver death (James 1:13–15).

James is like an Old Testament prophet, a tough voice bringing hard words that remind us that God's grace saves us from hell. Works don't save us, but they do show our faith—our belief that in following Christ, we have found the best, most meaningful, and ultimately satisfying way to live.

If Jesus isn't making a difference in the choices you make, in the actions you take, then James says you need to take a hard look at your faith. Is your trust in God or in yourself?

PRAY:

Father God, give me the strength to look at what I need to improve in my walk with You. I want Jesus' heart, desiring to please You above all else, knowing that Your love demonstrated the greatest humility and sacrifice. I can't do it without You, but with You I can do all things.

Seeking a Heart of Forgiveness

Read Hosea 3:1–5

KEY VERSES:

Israel will go a long time without a king or prince, and without sacrifices, sacred pillars, priests, or even idols! But afterward the people will return and devote themselves to the LORD their God and to David's descendant, their king. In the last days, they will tremble in awe of the LORD and of his goodness.
HOSEA 3:4–5 NLT

UNDERSTAND:

- *What is the deepest relationship wound you've ever suffered?*

- *What's the worst sin you've ever committed? Did you seek forgiveness?*

APPLY:

Hosea had one of the toughest assignments of all the Old Testament prophets: to marry a woman and have children, knowing she was going to cheat on him time and time again—the same way Israel kept stepping out on God by worshiping false deities.

Even though Hosea knew the pain was coming, he had a job to do. His ministry to Israel meant telling them about God's anger and coming punishment for their lack of faith.

When someone has wronged you, the first and hardest move is to forgive—whether or not you continue in relationship with that person. You can't do it alone. Invite trusted, godly men into your pain; ask them to listen, then to help pray you through it until you're ready to take that step of obedience and forgive that person.

If you're the causer of the pain, the pattern is similar: seek to make things right, putting the power to forgive in the other person's hands. Sometimes, that person won't want to make things right. Do all you can, and then trust God with the outcome.

PRAY:

Merciful God, I have carried a wound for a long time, and I'm struggling with it. I don't want to set myself up to be taken advantage of again, nor do I want to keep hurting others. Help me to see forgiveness the way You do, to trust in the healing You want for Your people.

The God Who
Wants to Know You

Read Acts 17:22–31

KEY VERSES:

"His purpose was for the nations to seek after God and perhaps feel their way toward him and find him—though he is not far from any one of us. For in him we live and move and exist."
ACTS 17:27–28 NLT

UNDERSTAND:

- *Looking back, how did God make Himself known to you?*

- *Are there areas of your life in which you tend to slip back into self-sufficiency instead of relying on God?*

APPLY:

The goal of religion is to tell us how we can find God. But Christianity comes at it the opposite way, revealing a God who comes to find us. His approach goes against our nature—our default setting is self-sufficiency: we want to save ourselves and be free to determine our own purpose.

Even so, we grasp intuitively that things aren't

the way they should be. The world's broken and unfixable, at least by us. Jesus is the fixer of all that is wrong with us and the world, and He wants to know you personally.

In Acts 17, Paul made it clear that the God the Greeks called *Unknown* is actually the God who made everything, who is bigger than any single set of beliefs, any idol, or any philosophy. And He is closer than we think, bestowing His common grace according to His good will to the just and unjust alike. He is a God of action and progress.

God's strange and wonderful purposes are fully displayed in Jesus Christ—God made flesh, who came to meet His own standards of righteousness and judgment, conquering the grave and sin so we could know Him personally. If that doesn't change the game for you, God remains unknown.

PRAY:

Almighty, All-Knowing God, thank You for making Yourself known to the world and to me. I want to live in the freedom and wisdom of being Your adopted son so I can know You more deeply and genuinely.

First Thoughts

Read Psalm 5:1–3

Key Verse:

*In the morning, O Lord, You will hear
my voice; in the morning I will prepare [a
prayer and a sacrifice] for You and watch
and wait [for You to speak to my heart].*
Psalm 5:3 amp

Understand:

• *How often do you praise God simply for being
who He is?*

• *How does the thought of God waiting to hear from
you in the morning make you feel?*

Apply:

Even if you're not a morning person, it's still a good
idea to focus on God first thing. It doesn't have to
be a full-on devotional or study (especially if you're
no good pre-coffee). Just talk to God as soon as you
can. A psalm of praise is a great way to offer God
your first thoughts.

It helps to do a little prep work the night before.
Find a Bible verse or passage you want to focus on,

then bookmark it so you can grab it the next morning and read it to God. You can read the verse as a prayer or use it as a launching pad for what comes to mind.

Then, take a moment of silence just to see if God impresses anything on your heart—a thought that you're reasonably sure came from Him and not you, a word of challenge or awareness, or even just a sense that it's good to seek God.

You can even do the same passage several days in a row to help fasten it into your memory and your heart. As a bonus, watch for ways in which God will repeat and confirm what you've read during the day or the week. He has His ways of letting you know His eye is on you and He sees what you're doing in faith each morning.

PRAY:

Thank You, Lord, for Your Word. I want to develop David's habit of turning my first thoughts over to You each morning.

Hope in the Darkness

Read Luke 22:39–46

Key Verses:

*"Father, if you are willing, remove this cup
from me. Nevertheless, not my will, but
yours, be done." And there appeared to him
an angel from heaven, strengthening him.*
Luke 22:42–43 esv

Understand:

- *What is the hardest moment God has ever allowed
  you to face?*

- *How did He eventually bring you comfort?*

Apply:

At Gethsemane, Jesus looked down the barrel of
God's wrath, the first and only time in His eternal
existence He would be separated from the perfect
community of the Trinity. He faced a darkness that
we as Christians will never have to—the eternal, dis-
solving misery of getting what we deserve as sinners.

And as a setup for that unbearable event, Jesus
couldn't even get His closest friends to pray with Him.
Another would turn Him over to the authorities, and

the crowds that lined His path with palm fronds a week earlier would be calling for His execution in a few hours.

If your heart aches thinking about that, let it ache. But then take comfort in knowing that Jesus understands darkness. Just as God sent an angel to comfort and strengthen Him, He will send comfort to you too in your darkest hours.

God asks us to do hard things at times and allows trials and troubles into our lives—not always because we've sinned but because He wants us to seek Him no matter what, to share in Christ's sufferings and then be strengthened with the hope He bought with His blood. The difference is that the separation from God we may feel is never actual distance. Jesus made sure of that.

PRAY:

I am humbled and awestruck by what You did for me, Lord Jesus. Thank You that the darkness You faced means that the darkness I face never gets the last word. Hardship affects me but doesn't define me. You do. I choose to die to myself today so I can follow You more closely.

Never, Never Give Up

Read Psalm 27:7–14

KEY VERSE:

I would have lost heart, unless I had believed that I would see the goodness of the LORD in the land of the living.
PSALM 27:13 NKJV

UNDERSTAND:

- *How do you feel when it seems like God is not answering your prayers?*

- *How do you usually look for God to work—in big ways or small ones?*

APPLY:

People bail on Jesus when the going gets tough. It was true 2,000 years ago, and it's true today. When He doesn't meet our expectations, we often look for a savior who matches our needs.

David saw the evil and cruelty in the world, recalled what he knew about God, and determined there was no one else worth trusting. He looked ahead to God's goodness in "the land of the living"—to the Messiah—and decided He was worth waiting on. At one point, in John 6:67–69 (ESV), Jesus even asked the Twelve if they were leaving Him too, and Peter said, "Lord, to whom shall we go? You have the words of eternal life, and we have believed. . .that you are the Holy One of God."

Knowing that God is working, even if it's behind the scenes, provides an anchor, a hope for those who believe. God never wastes pain. Every hardship, trial, and tear has purpose and meaning. The Bible lauds those who look beyond their immediate environment and trust in a kingdom yet to come—a creation restored and ruled with justice and compassion by the one who made it and then redeemed it. Don't lose heart. He is coming back, and He is here now, in the land of the living.

PRAY:

Sovereign God, I will wait on You. In this world of sin and suffering, I have still seen Your goodness and faithfulness. I will praise You, especially when I don't understand what You are doing. You are making all things new, and You will do what is right.

True Purpose

Read Ephesians 2:1–10

KEY VERSE:

*We are His workmanship, created in Christ
Jesus for good works, which God prepared
beforehand so that we would walk in them.*
EPHESIANS 2:10 NASB

UNDERSTAND:

* *How would you describe your purpose?*

* *How quick are you to follow God's leading? What,
if anything, holds you back from doing so as soon
as possible?*

APPLY:

The Greek word Paul used in Ephesians 2:10 for
workmanship is *poiema*, meaning "something made."
We get our English words *poem* and *poetry* from it.
Paul used it one other time, in Romans 1:20 (ESV),
when he noted that God's "invisible attributes, namely,
his eternal power and divine nature, have been clearly
perceived, ever since the creation of the world, in *the
things that have been made*" (emphasis added).

When God created the world, He poured His

eternal power and divine nature into all He made and called it good. You are an example of His finest work—the reason some translations of Ephesians 2:10 replace *workmanship* with *masterpiece*. Not only is God shaping and crafting you into a unique expression of His love and power, but He is brimming with purpose for you.

We are used to thinking of art as a result—a painting, a statue, a composition in words or music—that expresses something about the artist. And if God is the artist, the way He is sculpting you can only result in more than you can dream or imagine. You matter to your Maker, and nothing and no one can fulfill you like He can, and no one can delight Him the way you do. Listen for His calling, do everything for His glory, and enjoy all He has for you.

Pray:

God, You are the original artist, the great Creator.
You are the source of all beauty, goodness, and
truth, and Your purposes are higher and better
than anything the world can offer or humans can
imagine. Your glory resides in what's best for me.

Pain's Harvest

Read Hebrews 12:5–13

Key Verse:

No discipline is enjoyable while it is happening—it's painful! But afterward there will be a peaceful harvest of right living for those who are trained in this way.
Hebrews 12:11 NLT

Understand:

- *What qualities do you respect most in a mentor, coach, or teacher?*

- *What is your initial reaction to being redirected or challenged to improve?*

Apply:

The human capacity for endurance and pain tolerance is impressive, but it helps to have someone who's been there telling you what to expect, honing your skills, and encouraging you to press on. For the Christian, that's Jesus.

Jesus endured hostility and apathy, rejection and betrayal—culminating at the cross—because as Hebrews 12:2 (NKJV) says, He kept His eyes on the "joy that was set before Him": the goal of bringing as many people as would accept Him into the unity and harmony of relationship with God. He leaned into the brokenness of this world with the long-term goal of redeeming and restoring it, and He expects us to do the same. The pursuit of God revolves around letting Him teach us more about and guide us deeper into His truth, even and especially during painful times.

Hebrews 12:11 (NLT) offers a promise that God's chastening has a reward: "a peaceful harvest of right living for those who are trained in this way." Because of Jesus, we are part of the new covenant in His blood, bonded by His forgiveness and His promise to never leave or forsake us. Because of this, we can endure pain, knowing it will pass and that His eternal purposes are in it.

PRAY:

Father, I freely accept Your gift of adoption through Jesus Christ. I also accept the responsibilities of being Your son, of enduring the trials of this sin-broken world, and doing my best to keep Your ultimate goals of repentance, redemption, and restoration in mind. I trust You.

A Redeemed View of Sex

Read 1 Corinthians 6:12–20

KEY VERSE:

Flee from sexual immorality. Every other sin a person commits is outside the body, but the sexually immoral person sins against his own body.
1 CORINTHIANS 6:18 ESV

UNDERSTAND:

- *What old ways and habits of thinking about sex has God delivered you from?*

- *Why do you think sex is a different kind of temptation than, say, food or drinking?*

APPLY:

Sex is God's idea. It isn't inherently wrong or dirty. Whatever rules God set up for sex do need to be obeyed. His invention, His rules. When God established the boundaries for sex within the covenant of marriage, that's where He meant for it to happen—for unity, procreation, and pleasure.

In marriage, sex is the deepest expression of intimacy that is physically possible; it encompasses physical desire but also emotional need and spiritual harmony. Marriage means that a man and a woman have committed to being unified in every way (Genesis 2:24), including being a model of the unity and intimacy Christ desires with His Church (Ephesians 5:31–33).

So, when we're told to flee sexual immorality, it's because it represents a unique threat to our unity with God. First Corinthians 6:17 (NLT) says if you belong to Christ, you're His, body and soul, "one spirit with him." Few things require more discipline than sexual self-control, but do whatever you have to—confession, accountability, counseling, cold showers, device filters—to glorify God with your body. The level of suffering can be high, but not higher than the price God paid to make you His.

PRAY:

Heavenly Father, redeem my view of sex. Forgive me for the ways I've sinned sexually, treating my body as if it were mine alone. Give me the courage to do what I need to in this area, to bring all my thoughts into captivity to Christ.

Set Your Heart

Read 1 Chronicles 22:17–19

Key Verse:

"Now set your heart and your soul to seek the Lord your God. Therefore arise and build the sanctuary of the Lord God, to bring the ark of the covenant of the Lord and the holy articles of God into the house that is to be built for the name of the Lord."
1 Chronicles 22:19 nkjv

Understand:

- *What does it look like to give yourself completely to God? Name a few ways you do so.*

- *How do Bible study and worship help you put God first?*

Apply:

What David did in arranging for the temple to be built foreshadowed what God is doing now in the Church age. Instead of a single building and center of worship, however, God's presence and power are found in every individual who believes in the name of God's Son. Instead of drawing believers to a single place in Jerusalem, He is reaching the world through the gospel so voices from all nations can be raised in worship.

The heart of worship, however, remains the same: "Set your heart and your soul to seek the LORD your God." *Set* in Hebrew means to give with a determined purpose in mind. In context, it points to David's instructions to honor God wholeheartedly, to put Him first, and seek His help in building a place to honor Him above all else.

If you belong to Him body and soul, you're engaging in kingdom building. You're acting as His temple, bringing people to seek and worship God for themselves, some with refreshed hearts and others for the first time.

PRAY:

Lord, come soon. In the meantime, strengthen me to be focused on kingdom business— knowing You better, representing You well to others through acts of love, forgiveness, and kindness. I rejoice in Your faithfulness and set my heart and soul on seeking You today.

Do You Want to Be Healed?

Read John 5:2–9

KEY VERSE:

When Jesus saw him lying there and knew
that he had already been there a long time,
he said to him, "Do you want to be healed?"
JOHN 5:6 ESV

UNDERSTAND:

- *How did God answer the last big request you made of Him?*

- *When your prayers go unanswered or answered in a way you don't like, how do you respond?*

- *What does it mean to pray with expectation?*

APPLY:

Jesus cut right to the heart of the matter with the sick man at the pool of Bethesda: "Do you want to be healed?" Excuses are all he offered in reply—someone always beat him to the pool, no one helped him, and so on. What did Jesus know about this man that we don't?

Sometimes we get so used to a bad situation—a chronic illness or depression or anxiety—that we think God has lost interest in us. Or we think maybe God's grace isn't actually enough. God can handle honest doubt, but it's a mistake to hang onto doubt because we think it's all we have.

When God brings something like that to your attention, deal with it. If you can accept His redirection, no matter what it is, He will give you the grace and strength to move on. Let the Spirit guide you, bearing in mind Paul's words in Romans 8:26 (NKJV): "We do not know what we should pray for as we ought, but the Spirit Himself makes intercession for us."

PRAY:

Jesus, You know what's in my heart better than I do. You know why I slip up, especially in my attitude when I pray. Show me by Your Spirit why I'm struggling even to ask You for an answer. Give me the grace and strength to accept Your response, trusting who You are and what You know I need.

No Faking It

Read Zephaniah 2:1–3

KEY VERSE:

*Seek the LORD, all you humble of the land,
you who do what he commands. Seek
righteousness, seek humility; perhaps you will
be sheltered on the day of the LORD's anger.*
ZEPHANIAH 2:3 NIV

UNDERSTAND:

- *How do you show God that He has your
  whole heart?*

- *Does the thought of God's wrath scare you? Why
  or why not?*

APPLY:

Zephaniah's prophecies rained down hard, proclaiming "the day of the Lord" more than any other Old Testament prophet—God's wrath coming down through the ages on all who reject His ways. One particularly frightening warning comes in Zephaniah 2:3 (NIV): that if God's people will humble themselves, do what God commands, and pursue righteousness, "perhaps [they] will be sheltered on the day of the

LORD's anger." *Perhaps* they'll be sheltered? What's that about?

In Matthew 7:21–23, Jesus referred to people who call themselves Christians, and even behave like Christians, but will not be saved. They won't realize this until it's too late, when they are rejected by Jesus when He returns to judge the earth.

There's no room for *perhaps*, as Matthew 7:23 (MSG) cautions us: "All you did was use me to make yourselves important. You don't impress me one bit. You're out of here." Some men go to church for a long time before they actually become Christians.

Unless a man gives himself fully to God, letting his Maker do as He wants in his heart, he builds his life on sand. You know you're His when you'll give up anything to become more like Jesus, including coming clean and enduring temporary shame because you want to get right with Him.

PRAY:

Lord God, You are holy and righteous in all of Your ways. You want all of me because You gave me Your Son—Your highest and best—to save me. You held nothing back. Forgive me for the times and ways I haven't honored You by doing the same.

Chosen to Be Fruitful

Read John 15:9–17

KEY VERSE:

*"You did not choose Me, but I chose you and
appointed you that you should go and bear fruit,
and that your fruit should remain, that whatever
you ask the Father in My name He may give you."*
JOHN 15:16 NKJV

UNDERSTAND:

- *How do you think God defines love? How is His
  definition distinct from the typical human understanding of love?*

- *What does loving God look like to you?*

APPLY:

Jesus sets up His statement in John 15:16 by talking
about vines and branches (John 15:1–8). The analogy
establishes Jesus as the true vine, the source of eternal
life, and the Father as the vinedresser, determining
which grafted-on branches are fruitful and which
aren't. Once we are connected to God through Jesus,
our responsibility is to bear fruit—to obey God's
commands with humility and compassion.

In John 15:9 (NKJV) Jesus said, "Abide in My love." Clearly, God doesn't force our obedience. In that sense, we must cooperate with Him to fully work out His will for our lives. He knows who is going to receive His offer of salvation, but we still have to choose Him.

Jesus chooses to invest Himself in us, wanting to see us grow in godly love, and He tells us how to do so. In response, we obey His call to spread the good news to disciple those who respond to Jesus by choosing Him and lovingly serve others. That's God's definition of fruitfulness. As we abide in Christ, we are able to pray correctly, asking God in Jesus' name for things that are within His will and will bring Him glory.

PRAY:

God, You are love. It is out of the great and perfect love You have in the Trinity that You created people—so You could share it. You made us with free will so we could choose to love You, and You saved us from our warped, self-centered version of love by the blood of Christ.

Bringing God Your Broken Heart

Read Lamentations 3:17–26

KEY VERSE:

The LORD is good to those who wait [confidently] for Him, to those who seek Him [on the authority of God's word].
LAMENTATIONS 3:25 AMP

UNDERSTAND:

- *When bad things happen to people who reject God, what's your first reaction? What about when bad things happen to people who love God?*

- *Think of a time when God brought healing to your heartbreak.*

APPLY:

The prophet Jeremiah wrote Lamentations from a deep well of pain. God used him to warn Judah and Jerusalem for decades that judgment was coming if they didn't get right with the Lord. For his courage and faithfulness to his calling, he got utterly rejected.

But when his prophecies came true, Jeremiah didn't gloat. His heart broke, just like Jesus' did in

Luke 19:41–44, when He wept upon His triumphal entry into Jerusalem, knowing His chosen people didn't recognize Him and were about to reject and execute Him.

So, Jeremiah poured out his pain in a book. Lamentations is a brokenhearted cry after watching people suffer the consequence of rejecting God for so long that He eventually gave them what they wanted—to be left alone without His protection or comfort. It's like a preview of hell, and it should keep anyone who loves God from rejoicing in a sinner's downfall.

Yet, even in his lament, Jeremiah recalled God's faithfulness and mercy. It's just a few verses, but the impact is stunning—a man reminding himself (and us) that because God is who He is, there is hope in the midst of heartache. No moment is so dark that God's light can't shine in it. God will never abandon us.

Pray:

Lord God, the sorrows of my life and the heartbreak of the world overwhelm me. You don't owe me answers; I owe You everything. So I wait for Your hope.

Who's Lost?

Read Luke 19:1–10

KEY VERSE:

*"The Son of Man came to seek and
save those who are lost."*
LUKE 19:10 NLT

UNDERSTAND:

- *What led you to give your life to Jesus?*

- *How often do you fall back into acting like you don't
need Him? Do you recognize it when it happens?*

APPLY:

There's a part of us that says we're the ones pursuing
God—the ones who strive for holiness and righteousness, and God is there to reward us when we do. But
in reality, it's the other way around: God pursues us.
If He didn't come after us, we'd wander off into our
version of salvation, our own views of right behavior.

Remember who Jesus came to seek and save?
The lost. But He operated on a different definition
of *lost* than people were used to. Jesus was harshest
with those who seemed to have their act together—
the religious leaders of His day who felt they had

no need for the ministrations of some wandering preacher. But the truly desperate, the down-and-out, the empty-hearted, the poor and beaten-down knew real hope when they saw Him—and they latched on for dear life.

For some of us who, like Zacchaeus in Luke 19, think we've got it right most of the time, that awakening is sudden. But once Zacchaeus saw that Jesus knew him and still loved him, he wasted no time in trying to right his wrongs with others—and it started with God calling out to him. Own your lostness and Jesus will find you. Then leave your old futile days behind forever.

PRAY:

I trust You, Father. Thank You for coming to save me and not giving up on me when I resisted. Forgive me for the times I still resist, when I slip into self-sufficiency, and thanks for being faithful to teach me that I can't do life well on my own.

The Great Pursuit

Read Isaiah 65:1

Key Verse:

"I permitted Myself to be sought by those who did not ask for Me; I permitted Myself to be found by those who did not seek Me. I said, 'Here am I, here am I,' to a nation which did not call on My name."

Isaiah 65:1 NASB

Understand:

- *How did God pursue you to bring you to faith in Christ? Who or what did He use?*

- *How should you respond, knowing how relentlessly God has sought to make you His?*

Apply:

Story after story recounts God's pursuit of people's hearts, especially when they rejected Him and His ways. The Old Testament is primarily the story of how God picked out one old pagan guy and from him made a nation for Himself, preserving a lineage against all conceivable odds through which He would bring the Messiah and save the world.

Jesus is the face of God's great pursuit. He went

out of His way to visit Samaria because He had a divine appointment to bring hope and healing to a woman who had been rejected by her whole community. His parables contain images of shepherds leaving a whole flock to find one lost sheep, a woman scouring her entire house to find a lost coin, and a man selling everything to buy a single pearl worth everything to Him.

The theme? You matter to God. He reaches down to you so He can lift you up. You have purpose. God has prepared in advance good works for you to do, and as a Christian, you are now part of His chosen people. Surely His goodness, mercy, and unfailing love will follow you all the days of your life.

PRAY:

Thank You, Father, for never giving up on me.
I confess the times I've tried to run from You for
whatever reason. I want to know You more, to
connect with Your heart so You can use me to
connect others with Your astonishing love in Jesus.

When Good Things Go Bad

Read Luke 16:14–31

KEY VERSE:

"Abraham said, 'Child, remember that you in your lifetime received your good things, and Lazarus in like manner bad things; but now he is comforted here, and you are in anguish.'"
LUKE 16:25 ESV

UNDERSTAND:

- *How does the reality of heaven and hell affect the way you live?*

- *How often do you make time to check your priorities and make sure they line up with God's?*

APPLY:

In Luke 16, Jesus goes right from interpreting the Mosaic Law regarding marriage and divorce to the story of a rich man in hell. There's no indication that He shifted to a parable. It reads like a historical account; it feels real.

The story is not about rich people being inherently wicked or the poor innately good. Even though the possible glimpse into the workings of the afterlife is intriguing, that's not the point either. Jesus was driving at the unique power of His mission regarding one of the greatest worldly challenges to it: wealth and the power that comes from having money.

The story of Lazarus and the rich man is a stark illustration of the blinding power of wealth. If we have enough money, we hope we'll be able to avoid life's biggest problems. And money does help; it provides our daily bread and can be an equalizer for many injustices. But when a good thing replaces the best thing in our hearts, it becomes by definition a bad thing.

Unless God is our greatest desire, and our driving ambition is to know and serve Him, nothing will convince us that money and power won't do as well—not even someone rising from the dead.

PRAY:

Almighty God, the riches of Your kingdom are love, grace, mercy, and truth. The fruit of Your Spirit will last into eternity, fulfilled in our relationship with You in Christ and with others whom we help to know You. Anything else is fool's gold.

Love Never Quits

Read 1 John 4:15–21

KEY VERSE:

We love, because He first loved us.
1 JOHN 4:19 NASB

UNDERSTAND:

- *What do you think it means to truly love someone?*
- *How has God shown His love for you?*

APPLY:

Love originates with God; as 1 John 4:8 says, He is love. Father, Son, and Holy Spirit have always existed in perfect community and love—love so vital and abundant that God chose to create us to share in His love. There is nothing He could receive from us that would make Him greater, better, or more loving. In other words, He loves because it's who He is.

We are not born knowing how to love. In our natural, sinful condition, all we know is need. We need food, we need shelter, and we need love. More than anything, we want to be loved, and we learn to give love so we can get it. When we run into God's love—love that has everything to offer and nothing to gain from us—we don't know how to respond. It's not in us, but it can be taught as part of our new nature in Christ.

John gave us insight into loving like God loves. First, we have to accept what it cost for Him to love us—the cross. Once His Spirit is in us, though, His love begins to move in our hearts, pricking our conscience when we love in the old ways—selfishly, transactionally—and moves us to love others because we love Him.

PRAY:

Thank You for loving me before I ever loved You, God. I know I've made it hard at times, but You have relentlessly pursued me until Your love won me over. I want to love people today the way You love me—with patience and kindness, looking out for their highest good, especially when they make it hard.

The Mystery Revealed

Read Jeremiah 33:2–3, 14–16

KEY VERSE:

*"Call to me and I will answer you and tell you
great and unsearchable things you do not know."*
JEREMIAH 33:3 NIV

UNDERSTAND:

- *What has God done in your life that you never
imagined was possible?*

- *When God allows something hard you don't understand, what is your response?*

APPLY:

In the Bible, Paul used *mystery* to describe something
previously unrevealed—a matter of God waiting until
the right time to let us in on His plans. Nothing
mystical or self-contradictory, just a matter of God's
sovereignty and omniscience.

The Bible has a strong throughline, especially in
the Old Testament, of God's mysterious plan to save
humankind from sin. It unfolds gradually and spans
history, beginning directly after the fall, when God
predicted in Genesis 3:15 that a unique descendant

of Eve—the Seed—would crush Satan's head.

God told Jeremiah that if His people would look to Him, He would tell them "great and unsearchable things," specifically the mindboggling approach He was undertaking to deliver everyone—not just Jews but Gentiles too—from the just desserts of our sin. The Old Testament contains over 450 prophecies about the Messiah, some 300 of which were fulfilled during His earthly ministry.

We live now in the time the prophets looked forward to—the historical *anno Domini*, the era of our Lord Jesus. But there's more to come—the time of His return, reign, and restoration of creation, and eternity in the new heaven and earth beyond that. In Ephesians 1:9 (NIV), Paul described this as God making "known to us the mystery of his will according to his good pleasure, which he purposed in Christ." That's some mystery and some revelation—more than enough to keep waiting on God in faith as He works out the rest of the details.

PRAY:

God, Your timing is always perfect. Thank You for letting us in on Your astounding, counterintuitive plan of salvation. Lead and guide me into Your truth.

Life and Death on the Tip of Your Tongue

Read Proverbs 18:12–24

KEY VERSE:

*Words kill, words give life; they're either
poison or fruit—you choose.*
PROVERBS 18:21 MSG

UNDERSTAND:

- *Do you tend to say what's on your mind or do you
think before you speak?*

- *How often do you ask God to help you find the right
thing to say?*

APPLY:

Words either build or destroy, heal or harm. Wise
words satisfy like a good meal, but rash or foolish
words crush the spirit. Side effects include believing
lies about yourself and others and stuffing feelings
until they explode from your mouth and damage
hard-to-rebuild trust.

If you don't give authority over your tongue to
God, your words will be in a constant state of con-
tradiction. You will speak wisdom and foolishness

and bring light and darkness—often in the same conversation. But one word from God can change everything. His words can tell you where your own speech is driven by the wrong motives—ambition, aggression (and passive aggression), and apathy. As Proverbs 4:23 (NIV) says, "Above all else, guard your heart, for everything you do flows from it."

It's hard to find the right things to say if you're not familiar with the Bible. There is no substitute for God's own words of mercy and grace. The time you spend reading it, praying, and studying it is time spent stocking your heart with the vocabulary you need to control your tongue, filter out ungodly voices, and bring God's favor into your relationships.

PRAY:

Your Word is life, Lord God. You are the source of all wisdom and truth and the compassion and grace needed to deliver it so it lands well. May my words reflect a heart turned over to You, filled with Your Word. Make me quick to listen, slow to speak, and slow to anger. Holy Spirit, grow in me the fruit of self-control so I can master my tongue today.

Worth Every Loss to Gain

Read Matthew 13:44

KEY VERSE:

"The kingdom of heaven is like treasure hidden in a field, which a man found and covered up. Then in his joy he goes and sells all that he has and buys that field."
MATTHEW 13:44 ESV

UNDERSTAND:

- *Is there anything you would lose everything else over to keep?*

- *What does it mean to you that God considers you worth dying for?*

APPLY:

We often pass by God's kingdom without paying any attention to it. Maybe that's why many of Jesus' parables feature a field—in Matthew 13 alone, we have the sower, the wheat and tares, the mustard seed, and the hidden treasure.

We pass fields as we drive from city to city and from appointment to appointment. Unless we're farmers, we don't pause to think about what might be hidden beneath the ground. More immediate concerns command us, events and problems that reside in plain sight, and that's where our focus and energy go.

Jesus tells us in Matthew 6:33 to seek God's kingdom as the top priority in our lives. When we do that, He will provide everything we need to function well in life. Unfortunately, we can easily reverse our priorities, taking the kingdom for granted as we pursue our daily needs.

These parables also remind us of the joy of finding and being found. Jesus is the merchant looking for hidden treasure, keeping His plans a mystery until He sold Himself to accomplish His rescue mission. We are His treasure, His joy in giving all He has to win us.

Such love requires a response. Jesus gave up heaven to root in the dirt for us; what are we willing to lose to gain His kingdom?

PRAY:

Forgive me, Jesus, for all the times and ways I've taken Your pursuit for granted. You gave everything for my redemption. Help me to live with kingdom values embedded in my heart, putting You first in everything.

Do You Love to Worry?

Read Matthew 6:25–34

KEY VERSE:

*"Seek first the kingdom of God and
His righteousness, and all these
things shall be added to you."*
MATTHEW 6:33 NKJV

UNDERSTAND:

- *What worries you the most?*

- *How does worry affect your view of God?*

APPLY:

Nobody loves to worry any more than anyone loves
to pay taxes or have a root canal or host their in-laws
for a week. But those things need to be done, so we
do them. Maybe the real question is, do we love our
stuff more than we love God? The way we see God
affects the way we do everything else, especially worry.

When we lean into our troubles instead of God,
worry replaces worship; in effect, we're saying, "God,
I don't think You've got this." We would rather
trust our worry than His strength and provision.
Worry impacts our witness: Who wants to listen to

Christians who think their God isn't big enough to handle every problem?

Worry is a warning—a yellow light telling you that a choice is coming up fast. Choice one: take your worry and turn your concerns over to God, trusting Him to help you get through them. Or choice two: take your worry as a badge of honor, bravery in the face of God's apparent abandonment—a sign that you care more about your problems than God does.

Worry is a sign that you're paying attention, that you care about what's going on. That's good. But if you hang on to that worry, you risk making it an idol. So really, who do you love more, worry or God?

PRAY:

Lord, I confess my worrying to You. You know my needs well, but I keep forgetting Your all-powerful, all-knowing love, care, and mercy. Forgive me, and teach me to seek You first in every situation, especially the worrisome ones. I'll start by telling You what's on my mind today.

Getting Your Heart Straight

Read 1 Chronicles 16:7–14

KEY VERSE:

Look to the LORD and his strength;
seek his face always.
1 CHRONICLES 16:11 NIV

UNDERSTAND:

- *What generally happens when we forget who God is and what He has done?*

- *Do you make a regular habit of praising God?*

APPLY:

First Chronicles 16 centers on a long psalm (verses 8–36) that David and Asaph wrote as a response to God's greatness and mercies. That's so David, right? The guy was a psalm machine, always ready to burst into song about the Lord. So cool. But David's greatness really lies with his willingness to turn to God and face the music when he messed up. That's when the praise really counts.

When you become aware that you've gotten it wrong in God's eyes, it's easy to try and avoid Him.

You're embarrassed because you think you should know better, or you're mad because you think He is being too tough on you. Either way, you're not wrong. But don't let that keep you from coming to Him. And don't forget to start with praise.

Praising God is the only right move you have under every circumstance. Praise and worship are about Him, not you. He is the one who loves to forgive and reconcile and restore. He takes all your little brokennesses and makes a straight path back to Him—but you can't see it until you acknowledge Him.

Sing with gratitude for His mercies and faithfulness; sing because He deserves it no matter how you feel, and watch how your feelings will catch up with your faithful actions.

PRAY:

God, I am amazed by You. Please prepare my heart—the center of who I am, mind, body, and soul—to focus on You and let you know how great You are. Forgive me for my sin. Block out all my worries and thoughts so I'm only looking for You, only seeking to praise You.

Obedience Outside the Bubble

Read Philippians 2:12–18

KEY VERSES:

God is working in you, giving you the desire and the power to do what pleases him. Do everything without complaining and arguing, so that no one can criticize you. Live clean, innocent lives as children of God, shining like bright lights in a world full of crooked and perverse people.
PHILIPPIANS 2:13–15 NLT

UNDERSTAND:

- *What reasons, if any, make it difficult for you to share the good news?*

- *How mindful are you of God getting the glory for your words and actions?*

APPLY:

How often are you outside the Christian bubble? In other words, how much of your week do you spend out in the world—away from church and like-minded folks—surrounded by people of different beliefs and backgrounds? What's your attitude toward them?

How often do you catch yourself feeling superior to them? Do you let your standards slip because no other believers are around?

The key is obedience. Paul told the Christians in Philippi that it was even more important for them to obey God now that he, the founder of their church, wasn't among them. Philippians 2:12 (NLT) says we must "[work] hard to show the results of [our] salvation, obeying God with deep reverence and fear."

There's nothing passive about that work. We don't want to give people reason to think less of Him. People can be obnoxious about their objections to Jesus, the Church, and Christians in general, but it does no good to respond in kind. When you humble yourself like Paul did, you find the rhythm needed to represent Jesus well.

PRAY:

Jesus, if I just think about Your great love for me, demonstrated on the cross, I can see that there is a way to bring the truth to people outside my Christian sphere in a loving and respectful way. Help me to listen well and to speak with Your wisdom, insight, and compassion.

Vital Necessity

Read Jeremiah 29:10–14

KEY VERSE:

"Then [with a deep longing] you will seek Me and require Me [as a vital necessity] and [you will] find Me when you search for Me with all your heart."
JEREMIAH 29:13 AMP

UNDERSTAND:

- *What comforts you most about God's promises in Jeremiah 29:10–14?*

- *What does it take to make you search for God with "deep longing" and "as a vital necessity"?*

APPLY:

God's promises in Jeremiah 29 are familiar, but they go much deeper than the bumper-sticker context in which we normally see them. When Jeremiah passed these promises on to God's people, they were spiraling toward exile—the harsh, painful, uprooting consequences of their habitual hardheartedness and spiritual infidelity. But even after seventy years as refugees, most of them got comfortable in Babylon and didn't want to go back to Jerusalem.

Only a few hardy, obedient souls returned, and no bed of roses awaited them. They were forced to rely on God as a vital necessity—to feed them, help them rebuild their broken city, and keep their families safe from the angry pagans who had moved in while they were in Babylon. It was literally do or die.

Today, hostility toward God and Christians is on the rise as the culture wins major battles for people's hearts. A time of "vital necessity" and "deep longing" is coming because God is both faithful to see us grow and jealous to make us fully His. Better to move from a bumper-sticker faith to a more deeply reliant one now—something you're doing every time you dig into His Word.

PRAY:

Lord, will You make these well-known promises in Jeremiah 29 more real to me? I realize that's a dangerous prayer, one likely to push me out of my comfort zone, but I would rather have a deeper relationship with You in the trenches than a comfortable one with You at arm's length.

God Stories
Read 2 Corinthians 5:14–21

Key Verse:

He made Him who knew no sin to be sin for us, that
we might become the righteousness of God in Him.
2 Corinthians 5:21 nkjv

Understand:

- *What does God's grace mean to you in light of the*
  worst thing you've ever done?

- *What story would you tell someone of how God's*
  grace personally impacted your life?

Apply:

Because Jesus took on the ultimate pain of being cut
off from God, you will never be cut off from Him.
By His blood and with His strength, you can live
the life God wants you to, drawing on His power,
strength, and grace to be righteous, fully committed
to knowing Him better and bringing Him glory.

Because Jesus did what He did in the way He did
it, we should expect that anything is possible in this
life, both good and bad. The good points to God's
promise of life, but even the bad reminds us that

God's light will eventually extinguish all darkness. That's the power of grace.

Human history is full of stories of God's grace. What makes these accounts so powerful and poignant is the light shining through in the darkest possible moments—of God pursuing people in POW camps, penitentiaries, and sickbeds and delivering them from despair to hope. God has turned ashes into beauty through failed suicide attempts, averted abortions, horrible sicknesses, and the healing of unimaginable wrongs and insurmountable losses.

Dramatic or not, your God stories are one of your best tools when it comes to sharing the good news. God doesn't waste a drop of pain or sorrow, and He will use yours. Your suffering in His hands supercharges your faith.

PRAY:

Father God, I accept the hardship You allow in my life, knowing it strengthens my faith. Help me to learn what You're showing me and even to anticipate the impact it will have not just on me but on others who hear it and glorify You.

Lesser Gods

Read Romans 1:16–31

KEY VERSES:

*They knew God, but they wouldn't worship
him as God or even give him thanks. And they
began to think up foolish ideas of what God
was like. As a result, their minds became dark
and confused. Claiming to be wise, they instead
became utter fools. And instead of worshiping the
glorious, ever-living God, they worshiped idols.*
ROMANS 1:21–23 NLT

UNDERSTAND:

- *Based on Romans 1:16–31, what qualifies something as an idol?*

- *How often do you pray for individuals or groups
who really make you mad?*

APPLY:

The second half of Romans 1 is an unflinch-
ing description of why the world is so messed up.
Ultimately, idols exist because mankind has tried to
embody a greater sense of things into single facets,
individual representations of the divine that we can

wrap our minds around. We try to put God in a box and bring Him down to our finite level, resulting in corrupt, confused minds. In trying to limit Him, we shackle ourselves.

Things that are by themselves good—work, ministry, government and politics, even family—become idols when we make them supreme. When good things become the most important things, we settle for lesser gods, and they fail us constantly. What results is everything wrong with the world—all the hot button issues and every ugly sin in between.

It's easy to get angry at how badly we've broken what God made good. But being a new creation in Christ means we have to channel that anger into kingdom purposes. People are looking for ultimate meaning in their lives. You have it. Your role is to bring loving truth and truthful love into their day.

PRAY:

Lord God, I will not be ashamed of the gospel of Jesus Christ. You are the world's only hope, just as You are mine. Let me be salt and light, preserving Your truth and making Your grace and love known through kind words and bold deeds.

The Sweetness of Wisdom

Read Proverbs 24:13–14

KEY VERSE:

Know also that wisdom is like honey for you: If you find it, there is a future hope for you, and your hope will not be cut off.
PROVERBS 24:14 NIV

UNDERSTAND:

- *How often do you look to scripture when you need to make a decision?*

- *When has the wisdom of God's Word given you the same pleasure as a good meal?*

APPLY:

Solomon's point in Proverbs 24:14 seems simple: wisdom is sweet, just like honey. But there's more to this simple statement than meets the eye, and it starts with the sticky stuff. It helps to understand how honey was viewed in biblical times.

In ancient times, honey was considered to possess nearly magical qualities. It could be eaten raw or fermented into mead and honey wine and was also commonly used as medicine. Egyptians offered it in sacrifices to their gods and used it in embalming their dead. Civilizations going back thousands of years employed it to treat infected wounds and intestinal maladies. Science has since confirmed that honey contains antibacterial and anti-inflammatory properties with modern applications.

So, when God spoke of leading His people to a land flowing with milk and honey (Exodus 3:8), it suggests plentiful food but also a place of healing and well-being. God's desire to provide for us goes beyond meeting our basic needs; He also wants to draw us into the wonders of His wisdom.

That's what David meant when he wrote in Psalm 119:103 (NKJV), "How sweet are Your words to my taste, sweeter than honey to my mouth!" God's Word is the sweet treasure that enriches us, giving us wisdom and discernment to live as He intends.

PRAY:

Almighty God, thank You for Your Word. You keep Your promises, and I can trust You. Help me take Your words to heart, to obey You through good times and bad so I can experience the sweetness of Your truth, goodness, and provision.

Free Indeed

Read John 8:31–36

KEY VERSE:

"If the Son sets you free, you are truly free."
JOHN 8:36 NLT

UNDERSTAND:

- *What has Jesus set you free from?*
- *What things threaten to draw you back into captivity to the world?*

APPLY:

Every discussion, argument, and protest about rights comes down to freedom, which is commonly interpreted as the right to do whatever you want, to live "your truth" without hindrance or restriction. Look past whatever group is currently bugging you with such protests, and keep your eyes on the prize—living for Christ and filling and building the kingdom of God.

Only Jesus offers true freedom. What He has never offered, though, is an easy path to follow Him. He said in John 15:18 (NLT), "If the world hates you, remember that it hated me first." Luke 9:23 (ESV) says, "If anyone would come after me, let him deny himself and take up his cross daily and follow me." These are not statements of a trouble-free life. But then, the cross shows us that freedom isn't free.

Freedom carries responsibilities, primarily to honor and obey God. Psalm 119:45 (NLT) says, "I will walk in freedom, for I have devoted myself to your commandments." Pursuing God means obeying His Word, not because our salvation depends on it, but because we are responding to His love and grace. That's freedom's path.

In Christ, you are free from the pressures and expectations of the world. Christians are no longer bound by the limited, materialistic, transactional view of relationships. Our value is based on Christ's love for us, not our accomplishments, networks, or net worth. Use your freedom to help set others free.

Pray:

Lord Jesus, You have set me free for freedom's sake (Galatians 5:1). I am not bound to my old habits, the ways of the world, or the devil's lies. Give me the wisdom and power to live a life liberated from these things.

Do It for Love

Read Colossians 3:17–25

KEY VERSES:

*Whatever you do, work at it with all your
heart, as working for the Lord, not for human
masters, since you know that you will receive
an inheritance from the Lord as a reward.
It is the Lord Christ you are serving.*
COLOSSIANS 3:23–24 NIV

UNDERSTAND:

- *What motivates you in life? What gets you fired up?*
- *How do you decide if something is worth your effort?*

APPLY:

In Colossians 3, Paul brings a serious challenge for
Christian living, summed up in verse 17: do everything in Jesus' name. We tend to add the phrase to the
end of prayers like an automatic stamp of approval,
the proper sign-off, instead of realizing that every
time we talk to God, we are drawing on a seal of
approval guaranteed by Jesus' blood.

Jesus' name is our salvation; we can only approach
a holy God because He made it possible. But it should

also remind us John 3:16–style that Jesus did what He did out of love—love for the Father and for the world.

It's only possible to obey the list of examples in Colossians 3:18–23 because of Jesus' love. When you're thankful you can call on His name, it helps you be a loving husband, an engaged father, a concerned friend, and a worker with integrity. Or as Paul asked in Romans 2:4 (NASB), "Do you think lightly of the riches of His kindness and restraint and patience, not knowing that the kindness of God leads you to repentance?"

God did it all for love. We should too.

PRAY:

Thank You, Father, for Your patience with me. In my busyness, my ambition, my fear of missing out, I find myself forgetting that You are the one I'm doing it for—the one who makes any good thing worth doing, and worth doing Your way, with excellence in love, patience, and hard work. You gave Your best in Jesus Christ; You deserve my best in all I do.

Trouble's Always Knocking

Read Job 5:6–16

Key Verses:

"Trouble doesn't come from nowhere. It's human! Mortals are born and bred for trouble, as certainly as sparks fly upward. If I were in your shoes, I'd go straight to God, I'd throw myself on the mercy of God. After all, he's famous for great and unexpected acts; there's no end to his surprises."
Job 5:6–9 MSG

Understand:

* *How has God delivered you from trouble most recently?*

* *When bad news gets you down, how quickly do you seek God?*

Apply:

Our natural state causes trouble. Without God intervening and making Himself known, we'd just keep going in the wrong direction. Even Christians. Our soul is redeemed, but our flesh isn't yet.

Thankfully, God is not content to just leave us to the mess we've made. Jesus came to make salvation possible, and Revelation 21:1–4 describes the coming day when He will return and fix all of it, creating the new heaven and earth and eliminating death, sorrow, and pain.

In the meantime, though, our natural state is born for trouble; if there weren't any, we'd make some. That's why Job noted that pursuing God is our only hope in this life. God has never been content to let us suffer the consequences of our actions without remedy.

We still find evidence of His goodness all around us if we're looking. All we do in this life involves risk—love, work, friendship, and obedience to God. But He is just and good, and He is making all things new, now and in the forever to come.

PRAY:

Lord God, You have been incredibly merciful in light of our relentless drive to please ourselves rather than You. One day, You will make things right and good again, and our greatest pleasure and ambition will be pleasing You. Until then, I will seek to do so, with Your help. Trouble's always knocking, but I will let You answer.

Abide

Read 2 Chronicles 15:1–7

KEY VERSES:

"The LORD is with you when you are with Him. And if you seek Him, He will let you find Him; but if you abandon Him, He will abandon you. . . .[Be] strong and do not lose courage, for there is a reward for your work."
2 CHRONICLES 15:2, 7 NASB

UNDERSTAND:

- *What evidence do you have that God is sticking with you?*

- *In what areas or situations do you find it hardest to stick with God?*

APPLY:

In 2 Chronicles 15, God ensures His people that when they truly seek Him, they will find Him. It's a promise that is also a prophecy of Christianity. In Jesus, God lets Himself be found by us in an inclusive way that means He will never leave or forsake us. Put another way, His desire has always been to abide with us.

To abide is to remain in place. Jesus used *abide* memorably when He said in John 15:4 (NKJV), "Abide in Me, and I in you." We are to stay true to Him, remaining unified with Him primarily by obeying His singular command in John 13:34–35 to love one another as He has loved us. But as John 15:6 (MSG) says, failing to abide that way means we're "deadwood, gathered up and thrown on the bonfire."

Abiding is our responsibility under the new covenant in Jesus' blood. We love others as He has loved us so we can draw the lost to God's kingdom. As you abide in Him, enjoy the deep sense of purpose God has given you, and let it guide you in all you do.

PRAY

God Almighty, You are always faithful. I can trust You to stick with me no matter what. In response, I will abide with You, following Your commands to love out of love for You. Let Your purposes and ways fill me till I'm overflowing with them.

Depends on How You Ask

Read James 1:1–8

KEY VERSE:

If any of you lacks wisdom, let him ask of God, who gives to all liberally and without reproach, and it will be given to him.
JAMES 1:5 NKJV

UNDERSTAND:

- *When was the last time you had no idea what to do in a hard situation?*

- *How difficult is it for you to seek advice? Why?*

APPLY:

Have you ever been in a situation in which none of the standard decision-making protocols are working? Prayer isn't yielding a direction, listing the pros and cons reveals no clear option, the friends we consult are stumped, and our normal stress-reducing measures aren't helping. The fear of making the wrong choice paralyzes us.

Go back to prayer, though. What James makes clear is that the attitude with which we seek God makes all the difference. A tough choice is exactly the kind of trial that forces us to check our faith. Do we really believe what we say we believe about God, about prayer, about Him giving us what we need?

When you ask God for wisdom, don't hedge your bets—just think of what matters most to Him and then ask Him for help. James 1:5 assures you that God isn't going to look at you and say, "Dummy! It's about time." No, He is glad you're asking and will give you insight. Just make sure you're willing to line up your goals with His will.

The joy of seeking God doesn't come from having all the details sorted out but from remembering everything you know about your heavenly Father. He won't leave you hanging, but His response depends on your attitude about Him when you ask for His help.

PRAY:

Father, Your Word says so much about Your character—that You are good, faithful, and righteous. When I need Your wisdom, I am going to ask You for it. Please give me ears to hear and eyes to see Your response.

True Confession

Read 2 Kings 22:11–20

KEY VERSE:

*"Go, inquire of the LORD for me, for the people
and for all Judah, concerning the words of this
book that has been found; for great is the wrath of
the LORD that is aroused against us, because our
fathers have not obeyed the words of this book, to
do according to all that is written concerning us."*
2 KINGS 22:13 NKJV

UNDERSTAND:

- *What is your response when a passage of scripture
  convicts you of something?*

- *Who is affected most by your sin? What does confess-
  ing a sin to God mean to you?*

APPLY:

Today, some live as if the Bible were lost, but in King
Josiah's day, it was literally true. It wasn't until he
ordered repairs to the temple that a priest found a
copy of the Bible. When the king heard what God's
Word said, he tore his robes in dismay. Because of
the king's humble response, God said He would hold

back His just judgment until after Josiah's time.

Sometimes, God's Word holds a hard message for us. We need reminders that our sin, first and foremost, is against Him. We break His heart when we go our way instead of His. Others may suffer because of our choices, but we hurt God the most.

That's why the Bible reminds us to read it and to pray regularly, so we can be attuned to God. Our awareness and sensitivity to sin will increase, along with our willingness to confess it—to agree with Him that we've messed up. When we do, we are assured that He will take us back, that He won't cut us off as long as we remember who is on the throne.

PRAY:

Your mercies are humbling, Almighty Lord. You are justified in all Your judgments and correct in calling me out when I sin against You. I'm thankful that when I confess, You will wash me clean and restore me to right relationship with You.

The Paradigm Shift

Read Romans 3:10–26

KEY VERSES:

*"None is righteous, no, not one; no one
understands; no one seeks for God. All have
turned aside; together they have become
worthless; no one does good, not even one."*
ROMANS 3:10–12 ESV

UNDERSTAND:

- *Would you say that you are, generally speaking, a
good person? Why or why not?*

- *How would you describe the differences between
your goodness and God's?*

APPLY:

To establish his claim in Romans 3:23 that we all
sin and fall short of God's glory, Paul quoted Psalm
14, where David observed that no one is righteous
or wise enough to seek God. Because of our sin, God
is justified in His anger with the world and everyone
in it. That shocks people who think that being good
should be enough to get on God's good side.

Compared to God's holy standard of goodness,

however, there is no such thing as a good person. Of course, we all know people who are kind, decent, upstanding citizens. But humanity's version of good isn't enough to save us from our sin. When we relinquish the notion that people are inherently good in favor of faith in the good God who wants to save us all from ourselves, we undergo a paradigm shift.

Once you've shifted, you can fully embrace your true identity in Christ. This is part of what the oft-used phrase *the fear of the Lord* means—the humbling, awe-inspiring acceptance that God alone is God, and we must respond to Him, not the other way around. Then, He will help us love Him and others in ways that honor and please Him.

PRAY:

I'm so grateful, God, that You have made Yourself known to me. Knowing You has changed my life for the better because Your love teaches me to love the right way—with Your glory and the good of others as my highest goals.

Getting to Give
Read Luke 6:27–42

KEY VERSE:

*"Give, and you will receive. Your gift will
return to you in full—pressed down, shaken
together to make room for more, running over,
and poured into your lap. The amount you give
will determine the amount you get back."*
LUKE 6:38 NLT

UNDERSTAND:

- *What is your greatest challenge when it comes
to giving?*

- *How does God demonstrate His attitude
about giving?*

APPLY:

Based on what Jesus is saying in Luke 6, it's clear
that in God's economy, money isn't just about money.
He was discussing the right *attitude* toward money—
lending to those in need without expecting repay-
ment and giving out of compassion, not just doing
smart business. Jesus sets up His idea of giving by
challenging us about our inherent judgmentalism
and hypocrisy. Wait—what?

It's a brilliant setup because it reveals the ungodliness of our default setting about giving. We give to get. We give to the needy because it makes us feel good about ourselves, or it's a tax write-off, or it reinforces our sense of superiority. In other words, we judge ourselves and others based on how generous we are. Thankfully, God doesn't judge us based on what we can give Him. He just wants us.

The image in Luke 6:38 is of a measure of grain—a daily allotment—shaken and pressed into the measuring cup so that it can't hold a single grain more and runs over. That's how God has blessed you in Christ: giving you His very best so you couldn't possibly feel shortchanged by His blessing. And that's how He wants you to be in your giving—joyfully meeting others' needs because your cup is overflowing with His love, grace, and provision.

PRAY:

Father God, I ask for Your wisdom in untangling my thoughts about money and giving and how closely they are related to judging others. Help me to see others the way You see them—as being worth the highest cost to seek and to save.

Open Arms and Unmerited Mercies

Read Psalm 51:1–6

KEY VERSES:

You're the One I've violated, and you've seen it all, seen the full extent of my evil. You have all the facts before you; whatever you decide about me is fair. I've been out of step with you for a long time, in the wrong since before I was born. What you're after is truth from the inside out.
PSALM 51:4–6 MSG

UNDERSTAND:

- *How hard is it for you to seek God when you've sinned?*

- *How often do you condemn yourself instead of seeking God's forgiveness?*

APPLY:

David wrote Psalm 51 after Nathan busted him for committing adultery with Bathsheba, then arranged for her husband, Uriah (one of his most loyal soldiers), to die at the frontlines of a battle at which David wasn't present. Once David saw his actions through God's eyes, his heart broke, and he penned this famous psalm of repentance.

How could David turn so wholeheartedly to God after messing up so badly? Rather than asking that question, we're better served to see something bigger and deeper than David's sin—we need to grasp his view of God.

God hates sin because it separates us from Him. He knows we can't repay the cost, but His perfect love demanded that He pay that painful price Himself. He is always standing nearby, wanting to pull you into a loving embrace of forgiveness and peace. The depth of your wretchedness can't match the greatness of His love.

Like David, you're worse than you can even imagine and more loved than you can ever dream. Forgiveness and restoration begin when you get out of your head and trust in His love for you.

PRAY:

Holy and merciful Lord, I've too often ignored Your love, Your willingness to forgive and restore me. I'm so sorry. Please help me to see You not as my fear dictates but as You are—arms open, waiting for me to turn back to You.

Getting Righteousness Right

Read Matthew 5:3–10

Key Verse:

"Blessed are those who hunger and thirst for righteousness, for they shall be filled."
Matthew 5:6 nkjv

Understand:

- *When you read the Sermon on the Mount, what challenges you?*

- *What is the difference between God's righteousness and the human version?*

Apply:

The challenge of hungering for righteousness is that we don't hunger for what we don't think we need. But over and over, the Bible talks about the importance of righteousness. We are to pursue it, practice it, do it, walk in it, and suffer for it. But before any of that, we must become it. All the right behavior in the world doesn't make us right with God.

The more we grasp our need for Jesus, the more we see the value of His righteousness: humbling

Himself to do the dirty work required to save us and standing for what matters to God when it cost Him His reputation. Because Jesus had right standing with God, He wanted to obey, and He had the courage to do God's will. Thus, His suffering only strengthened His resolve.

Suffering can clarify your priorities because it makes you desperate enough to see what really matters. On our own, we can't be humble or hungry or merciful enough, can't mourn our wretched state enough, can't think or speak or behave purely enough to get into God's kingdom.

But Jesus' righteousness is enough. The Beatitudes should lead you to the end of yourself; but when you get there, you'll see all that God has offered you in Jesus.

PRAY:

Jesus, thank You for being perfect in righteousness so I could receive Your right standing with God. I'm asking You to show me anything in my life that threatens me knowing You better. Even when it hurts, I want to be more like You because I know You are the way, the truth, and the life.

Seeking Next Steps

Read Ezra 8:21–23

KEY VERSES:

We had told the king, "The hand of our God is for good on all who seek him, and the power of his wrath is against all who forsake him." So we fasted and implored our God for this, and he listened to our entreaty.

EZRA 8:22–23 ESV

UNDERSTAND:

- *What kind of situation compels you to fast as you seek God?*

- *Why does denying yourself help you to follow God more confidently?*

APPLY:

Ezra was a priest who led a small group of courageous volunteers on a dangerous journey out of exile and back to Israel. The odds were against him, but he had made a stand—a strong statement of faith to the king that God would see them through. Realizing what a struggle lay before him and all those God had entrusted to him, he wisely turned to God with prayer and fasting.

The combination of prayer and fasting leads to powerful results. When you hunger for God more than for food, you can grasp what David experienced in Psalm 63:1, 3, 5 (NIV): "You, God, are my God, earnestly I seek you; I thirst for you, my whole being longs for you. . . . [M]y lips will glorify you. . . . [And] I will be fully satisfied as with the richest of foods."

Trusting God to the extent that you deprive yourself helps you to see the situation through God's eyes, and that often leads to Him showing you what to do next. It's not usually a linear path, but it's the path God wants you to travel. Fasting and prayer have a humbling effect that put you in the right frame of mind to follow Him where He leads.

PRAY:

Heavenly Father, I don't want to be on any path but the one You set before me. I trust You with the situation before me now, and I understand that fasting and prayer open my heart to receive my next step from You.

When Grace Is All You've Got

Read 2 Corinthians 12:7–10

KEY VERSES:

At first I didn't think of it as a gift, and begged God to remove it. Three times I did that, and then he told me, My grace is enough; it's all you need. My strength comes into its own in your weakness. Once I heard that, I was glad to let it happen. I quit focusing on the handicap and began appreciating the gift.
2 CORINTHIANS 12:8–9 MSG

UNDERSTAND:

- *Has God allowed a recurring challenge in your life? What might He be doing through it?*

- *When has God shown up strong in a moment of weakness for you?*

APPLY:

When Jesus brought Paul into the fold, the former Pharisee had some catching up to do. Paul had been a zealous legalist and Christian terminator, so, as 2 Corinthians 12:1–6 tells us, Jesus took him on personally, preparing him for service.

God used that unspecified physical/spiritual ailment to educate Paul about the sufficiency of His grace. When God refused to remove it, Paul surrendered any sense of entitlement, markers of status, or worldly success. As a result, God's grace—His abiding power and favor in the face of hardship—enabled Paul to endure a staggering checklist of missionary suffering (see 2 Corinthians 11—yikes!)

So, when Paul said in 2 Corinthians 12:10 (MSG) that he had learned to "take limitations in stride," he meant it. Revisit your worst moments—the times when all seemed lost and none of your experience, talents, or skills were enough to fix the problem. Jesus was there, and by His grace you persevered.

PRAY:

Lord Jesus, compared to Your strength, all else is feeble and small. That includes all the obstacles You allow into my path, all the valleys You walk me through, all the times I fail miserably—they don't get the final word. You do, and that is enough for me.

God Has the Final Word

Read Romans 8:28–39

KEY VERSES:

[God's Spirit] knows us far better than we know ourselves, knows our pregnant condition, and keeps us present before God. That's why we can be so sure that every detail in our lives of love for God is worked into something good.
ROMANS 8:27–28 MSG

UNDERSTAND:

• *What is the worst thing you can think of happening to you? Why might God allow it?*

• *Have you ever mistaken God's sovereign perspective for disinterest or even dislike?*

APPLY:

Being a Christian means being persuaded of the joy, relief, and comfort that come from being right with God—to the extent that tribulation doesn't shake us. We receive His blessings as coheirs with Christ, along with the power to pass through the troubles that come with this world rather than getting stuck in them.

Romans 8:28 is so well known that we can forget

its power. God causes *everything* to work together. Take the proper view of God's role in your life. He is there at the beginning, waiting for you to respond to your calling in Christ, and He is there along the way, working all things together for good. And you can be sure He will be with you in the end.

When hard times come, let God have the final word, as Paul did in Romans 8:29–30 (NLT): "God knew his people in advance, and he chose them to become like his Son, so that his Son would be the firstborn among many brothers and sisters. And having chosen them, he called them to come to him. And having called them, he gave them right standing with himself. And having given them right standing, he gave them his glory."

PRAY:

Father, I give You the final word in my life. I believe what You say about me—that I am Your son, that You are for me, and that You are changing me into the image of Jesus.

Don't Go with the Flow

Read 2 Chronicles 17:3–10

KEY VERSES:

The LORD was with Jehoshaphat, because he walked in the earlier ways of his father David. He did not seek the Baals, but sought the God of his father and walked in his commandments, and not according to the practices of Israel. Therefore the LORD established the kingdom in his hand.
2 CHRONICLES 17:3–5 ESV

UNDERSTAND:

- *What is your natural tendency—to go along to get along or to risk offending people with God's truth?*

- *When have your feelings won out over your knowledge of God?*

APPLY:

Israel's history is stained with the spiritual affairs God's people had with lesser gods and ways of living—telling Him repeatedly with their hardhearted actions, "You aren't enough for me; You don't make me happy anymore."

Sadly, they forgot the fear of the Lord. Little by

little, they stopped doing the things that promoted healthy respect and awe for God, His Word, and His ways. Infidelity, whether it's marital or spiritual, results from dozens of small decisions that break trust, mixed with all our indulged resentments. Eventually, we'll cross the line one way or another. Spiritually, the only difference is that God is never at fault. We keep Him at arm's length, acting like we love better or know more about our needs than He does. In the name of pursuing happiness, we forsake righteousness.

To avoid slipping away from God, cultivate your relationship with Him. Consider how Jehoshaphat broke sin's cycle in 2 Chronicles 17: fear the Lord, seek His ways in His Word, then do them. Don't chase your feelings or go with the flow; what's easy is seldom what's right.

PRAY:

Lord, You know if there are any areas in my heart I'm setting aside from You for something lesser. I know that if I'm right with You, I will be able to resolve issues in my other relationships in ways that please and honor You.

In It for the Glory

Read John 17:1–10

KEY VERSES:

"Father, the hour has come; glorify your Son that the Son may glorify you, since you have given him authority over all flesh, to give eternal life to all whom you have given him. And this is eternal life, that they know you, the only true God, and Jesus Christ whom you have sent."

JOHN 17:1–3 ESV

UNDERSTAND:

- *What does the word* glory *make you think of?*

- *Why do you think Jesus was so focused on bringing glory to God and Himself?*

APPLY:

When Jesus asked the Father to restore Him to His proper place of glory, He was signaling more than the successful end of His mission on earth. He was also describing our path forward as believers: the Son glorified the Father through His obedience at the cross, and the Father glorified Him in return by raising Him from death and restoring Him to heaven, we who believe in Jesus will also be glorified.

Jesus did all He did so God would receive glory. When in John 11:4 (ESV) He raised Lazarus, it was for "the glory of God, so that the Son of God may be glorified through it." And Jesus signaled His own impending death by telling His disciples in John 12:23 (NASB), "The hour has come for the Son of Man to be glorified."

That same glory is ours now, fueling us to do our best to honor God in response to His grace and love. His glory includes the way we honor Him when we suffer, the same way Jesus honored His Father by taking the cup. Your perseverance in hard times and your gratitude in peaceful ones bring Him glory.

PRAY:

Father, Son, and Holy Spirit, You alone deserve all glory and honor. It blows my mind that Your plan in saving me was so I could share in Your holy glory. Let everything I think, say, and do today be focused on making Your name great.

Even When You Don't Get It

Read Isaiah 45:9–12

KEY VERSE:

"What sorrow awaits those who argue with their Creator. Does a clay pot argue with its maker? Does the clay dispute with the one who shapes it, saying, 'Stop, you're doing it wrong!' Does the pot exclaim, 'How clumsy can you be?'"

ISAIAH 45:9 NLT

UNDERSTAND:

- *When have you felt like God let you down or seemed far away when you needed Him?*

- *What is your perspective on that time now? Did God teach you anything about Himself or yourself?*

APPLY:

Sometimes, we feel like God lets us down. A heartfelt prayer goes unanswered, or we don't like the answer we get—and we double down on what we want, feeling shortchanged, rather than asking if God might have something different for us. In those moments, we forget that faith is about trust.

When disappointed, our default reaction is to make it about us, thinking we know better than God. Even as Christians, our flesh still resists the idea of having a master. Jesus busted us when He asked in Luke 17:9–10 (NLT), "Does the master thank the servant for doing what he was told to do? Of course not. In the same way, when you obey me you should say, 'We are unworthy servants who have simply done our duty.'"

Pursuing God means that when God disappoints you, He is still God to you. No matter what you accomplish in this life, He will always be the boss and you, an unprofitable servant. But by His grace you are a beloved adopted son, freed from depending on worldly outcomes to make you secure and valued. Set your expectations accordingly.

PRAY:

Lord God, I admit there are times when I just need to get over myself, especially when it comes to my attitude toward You. Forgive me for giving You lip service while I keep my heart closed to Your holiness. Thank You for being patient to finish what You started with me.

The Only Right Response
Read Romans 11:33–12:2

KEY VERSES:

Therefore, I urge you, brothers and sisters, in view of God's mercy, to offer your bodies as a living sacrifice, holy and pleasing to God—this is your true and proper worship. Do not conform to the pattern of this world, but be transformed by the renewing of your mind. Then you will be able to test and approve what God's will is—his good, pleasing and perfect will.
ROMANS 12:1–2 NIV

UNDERSTAND:

- *What have you sacrificed to follow Jesus?*

- *How has knowing God transformed the way you think, speak, and act?*

APPLY:

Paul opens Romans 12 with *therefore*, an invitation to view what he will say next through the lens of what he just established in Romans 11, where he detailed God's plan for Israel in light of the gospel. His point? God's knowledge and wisdom are deeper than the Mariana Trench. He made everything, holds it together with His will, and His creation sings His praises.

God is who He is: holy and majestic, all-knowing and all-powerful, fully present in every moment and place, good and loving and just. Therefore, the only proper response is to give ourselves completely to Him—to offer our bodies as a living sacrifice.

Knowing Him personally transforms us from death to life, selfish to selfless, judgmental to gracious. Any sacrifice we might make pales next to what He has done, particularly at the cross. And His reward for our total commitment to Him is life to the fullest, now and in eternity.

PRAY:

*Almighty God, You alone deserve all praise
and glory. It is the honor of my life to lay down
everything I am and have for Your sake. I forsake
my rights, my accomplishments, my dreams
so I can realize Your plans for me, which are
part of a story that is greater and higher and
more wonderful than I can even imagine.*

Trust Fall

Read Proverbs 3:3–6

KEY VERSES:

Trust GOD from the bottom of your heart; don't try to figure out everything on your own. Listen for GOD's voice in everything you do, everywhere you go; he's the one who will keep you on track.
PROVERBS 3:5–6 MSG

UNDERSTAND:

- *Think of a time when God showed you the right path in His Word.*

- *How often do you seek God in His Word when you face a difficult challenge?*

APPLY:

The most dominant philosophy today is this: what you think is true is what matters most. To refute another's claim to what's right or even to ask questions is the same as attacking that person's core identity. The idea of objective truth—facts, ideas, ethics—that holds true for every person in every culture is, to say the least, out of fashion. But God's words never lose their power or relevance, so He defines what matters most.

Trusting God means not leaning on your own understanding. If God made all your paths straight before you ever set out, you wouldn't need to trust Him. The bumps, twists, and turns, the dark alleys, and flat tires—these are all chances for you to look to God for wisdom and help. And He will not let you down.

If you aren't regularly reading God's truth and applying it to how you live, the world's views will replace God's wisdom. Let His words change your default setting from self-sufficiency to God-dependency. Trade in the world's lesser gods for the wisdom and guidance of the one true God. Lean into Him; He won't let you fail.

PRAY:

Jesus, You are the Word of God. No one is greater than You. As Peter said in John 6:68 (AMP), "Lord, to whom shall we go? You [alone] have the words of eternal life [you are our only hope]." I bring my praise, questions, and troubles to You. Lead me in the way I should go.

Good Trouble

Read John 5:24–30

KEY VERSE:

"I can of Myself do nothing. As I hear, I judge; and My judgment is righteous, because I do not seek My own will but the will of the Father who sent Me."
JOHN 5:30 NKJV

UNDERSTAND:

- *Have you ever gotten in trouble for doing the right thing?*

- *Based on Jesus' interactions with people, what matters most to God?*

APPLY:

Jesus made trouble. He tipped apple carts (and temple tables) regularly, rolling everyone's rotten fruit right out in their paths. He claimed sin, evil, and hell were real, along with other divisive claims, and He owned it in Luke 12:51 (NKJV): "Do you suppose that I came to give peace on earth? I tell you, not at all, but rather division."

If we want to truly know Jesus, we must accept all of Him—not just the love and mercy but the unrelenting zeal for God's glory and the disquieting holiness of His words and claims. Jesus fully represents God, both the grace and the wrath, the stunning humility required to save us and the unswerving confidence that His judgment is just. We can't pick and choose with Jesus.

We want to live up to Jesus' high expectations because He saved us, not so we can be saved. That means we can do what's right, enjoying the fruits and enduring persecution because we know our salvation doesn't depend on it. We are free to speak truth lovingly and to love truthfully. That is God's will, expressed perfectly in Jesus. If we can limit our offenses to the gospel, we'll still get in trouble, but it will be the good kind.

PRAY:

Jesus, You met Your own holy requirements—fully God and fully man, a perfect, spotless sacrifice—and gave Your life for mine. Thank You for showing God's gracious and patient heart through all You said and did. I hear Your voice and I am Yours. Help me to represent You well to others.

Performance Anxiety

Read Isaiah 58:1–14

KEY VERSES:

"This is the kind of fast day I'm after: to break the chains of injustice, get rid of exploitation in the workplace, free the oppressed, cancel debts. What I'm interested in seeing you do is: sharing your food with the hungry, inviting the homeless poor into your homes, putting clothes on the shivering ill-clad, being available to your own families."

ISAIAH 58:6–7 MSG

UNDERSTAND:

- *What do you think the purpose of fasting is?*

- *Do you ever catch yourself performing like a Bible-believing Christian instead of just being one?*

APPLY:

God's message in Isaiah 58 criticizes those who act in ways that seem religious but completely miss the point—fasting and praying, for instance, should lead to compassionate behavior toward others for their good, not "Hey, look how super holy I am, everyone!"

Performance is often a protective mechanism.

Church can be the most judgmental place on earth. Everyone goes through hard times, but when we get to church, the masks go up. Any problems get back-burnered in the one place they should be safest to discuss, where grace and loving truth are supposed to be our calling cards. To love like Jesus does is to accept that everyone struggles, even us. We own our shortcomings, give them up to God, forgive and seek forgiveness, and then show His grace to others.

Then when we pursue God through fasting and prayer, we'll hear God clarify who He is, which helps us know what we should do and how we should love others. When what He thinks matters most, then we will find our joy in Him and He will guide, protect, provide, and prepare us for His good work—no faking required.

PRAY:

*Lord, I want to honor You in everything
I do. Forgive me for the times I've slipped
into acting like a good Christian instead of
just being one. I want to use everything You
have given me for Your glory, not mine.*

Know Your End Times Stuff

Read Luke 21:5–38

Key Verses:

"Watch out! Don't let your hearts be dulled by carousing and drunkenness, and by the worries of this life. Don't let that day catch you unaware like a trap. For that day will come upon everyone living on the earth. Keep alert at all times. And pray that you might be strong enough to escape these coming horrors and stand before the Son of Man."
Luke 21:34–36 nlt

Understand:

- *How well do you understand the biblical conditions for the end times?*

- *Does waiting for Jesus to return make you want to check out and wait or engage more fully in His work?*

Apply:

The end times are always a hot topic both in and out of the Church. We know Jesus is coming back and will fix everything when He does—pause for a hallelujah!—but when? How long, Lord?

In Luke 21, Jesus offers a number of predictions about the end times. Some of them have already been fulfilled, and others describe prefulfillments—wars, uprisings, false messiahs, persecution for believers—that are only signs of similar, greater-scale conflicts that will come at the end of days.

The details Jesus spoke of are well worth studying if only because He told us to in Revelation 1:3. Every generation has had reason to believe the last days are at hand. This one is no different—although, seriously, this could be it! But just as important as knowing about the last days is living in light of them. Make each day count while this age of grace lasts.

PRAY:

Father, as I look at the madness of the world, help me to fight the desire to check out. I want to be able to speak Your truth in a world where people are losing hope. Give me the strength to stay engaged and involved in the sphere of influence You have given me. Come soon, Lord Jesus!

Peace in Troubled Times

Read Habakkuk 3:17–19

Key Verses:

Though the fig tree may not blossom, nor fruit be on the vines; though the labor of the olive may fail, and the fields yield no food; though the flock may be cut off from the fold, and there be no herd in the stalls—yet I will rejoice in the LORD, I will joy in the God of my salvation.
Habakkuk 3:17–18 nkjv

Understand:

- *What are your hardest struggles today?*
- *Think of God's track record with you. How has He delivered you in the past?*

Apply:

When you read Habakkuk's description of his hard times, try to put it in terms of the challenges you're facing—with your marriage, job, or kids, for example. How do you say that last line and mean it? When nothing good is happening in your life, how do you get in touch with God's goodness?

In Habakkuk 3:2 (AMP), the prophet said, "O

Lord, I have heard the report about You and I fear. O Lord, revive Your work in the midst of the years." He remembered what God had done in His history with Israel, bringing blessing and, when needed, judgment to bring repentance and restoration. God doesn't forget or abandon His people, no matter how bleak their outlook seems. You are not alone, and you never will be.

When Jesus said He is the bread of life, He meant that He alone could satisfy our deepest needs—deeper than job satisfaction, than fulfilling human relationships, than hunger itself. Though your situation may be dire, He will lift your head in expectation of what He will do.

Pray:

God, I confess that I often expect You to answer my prayers my way. Help me to leave room for You to answer them Your way. You know everything, You are faithful, and You are working all things together for my good and Your glory. I trust You with my troubles.

When the Critics Come

Read 1 John 1:5–10

Key Verse:

*If we confess our sins, He is faithful
and just to forgive us our sins and to
cleanse us from all unrighteousness.*
1 John 1:9 nkjv

Understand:

- *What is your typical first reaction to criticism?*

- *Reread 1 John 1:8–10. What do you have in
common with all critics, regardless of their intention
or accuracy?*

Apply:

It's hard to admit you're wrong. No one likes being
criticized. Whether the comment has merit or not,
it feels unfair and unjust. You're busy enough trying
to do your best without these stings and arrows. So,
how do you deal with criticism?

First, you have to ask the right question—which
isn't *Why am I being attacked?* but *Why does this attack
bug me so much?* Whenever those irritable feelings crop
up and make you mad, you are reacting out of pride,

as 1 John 1:8 suggests. You can't control the other person's attack, but you can mind your response. And the best way to do that is to go plank-eye with the criticism (Matthew 7:3), checking yourself to see if there's even a sliver of truth. You might, for instance, have been criticized because you made a good point with a graceless tone.

It's also possible, especially with a critic who doesn't know you, that you're being criticized for a view you don't hold. But even if the critic is totally wrong, you have to go back to times you've spoken imperfectly, carelessly, hastily and let that humble you toward grace and prayer. Remember, confession and forgiveness apply to you first.

PRAY:

*Father, forgive me for bristling at criticism
and resorting to counterproductive reactions.
Help me to seek to convince others without
condemning them, to build them up instead of
knocking them down. I am so grateful that when
I confess my sins, You are faithful to forgive me
and set me back on Your path of righteousness.*

Lifted Up in the Chaos

Read Isaiah 40:27–31

Key Verses:

Even youths shall faint and be weary, and young men shall fall exhausted; but they who wait for the LORD shall renew their strength; they shall mount up with wings like eagles; they shall run and not be weary; they shall walk and not faint.
ISAIAH 40:30–31 ESV

Understand:

- *What do you do when you feel worn out by the world?*

- *When you read Isaiah 40, what stands out to you about God?*

Apply:

The first thirty-nine chapters of Isaiah center on God confronting Israel for trusting in kings and nations rather than their true King, God Himself. So, it's a refreshing surprise when Isaiah 40:1 (NKJV) shifts gears: "'Comfort, yes, comfort My people!' says your God." He chastens His people for their own good, but He also redeems His people from their trouble.

In verse 3 (NKJV), Isaiah predicts the coming of Christ—the focal point of redemptive history, heralded by John the Baptist: "The voice of one crying in the wilderness: 'Prepare the way of the LORD; make straight in the desert a highway for our God.'" And in verse 4, God's healing methods are poetically described—valleys lifted up, mountains brought low, crooked places straightened, and rough ground leveled—forecasting the miraculous work Jesus did in His ministry to bring redemption, restoration, and holiness.

In this chaotic, selfish world, we must not lose hope. God is aware of the injustices we have done and those done to us, and He is setting them right. When the world exhausts you, when you're sick of the sin still evident in yourself, don't give up. God has more than enough power to lift you up.

PRAY:

*Almighty God, faithful and true, You deserve
all the praise and thanks. The world surrounds
me, overwhelms me with cruelty and chaos and
conflict—but You are making all things new,
starting with me. You are my strength and
shield, my hope, and all I truly want or need.*

On Equal Footing

Read Galatians 3:26–29

Key Verse:

There is neither Jew nor Greek, there is neither slave nor free, there is neither male nor female; for you are all one in Christ Jesus.
Galatians 3:28 NKJV

Understand:

- *What types of people or situations tempt you to have an attitude of superiority?*

- *How does the knowledge that all people stand equally before God affect your treatment of others?*

Apply:

Everyone longs to be loved and highly valued. We have these desires because we're made in God's image; therefore, only He can meet them. Our sinful tendency is to think we know better than our Maker what is best for us. But our best thoughts should turn us toward God, not from Him.

When we reject God, we can no longer see His truth, beauty, or goodness. Without His protective boundaries and limits, anything is possible—and that's not good. Any earthly minded institution or philosophy moves us not toward freedom from what truly shackles us—sin and its consequences—but *from* accountability *to* a power higher than ourselves.

Both religion and secular humanism give false context and misinterpreted facts to justify judgmentalism and segregation. The horrors that result from putting this belief into action—racism, genocide, terrorism, war, and eugenics, among others—offer a foretaste of hell.

Before God, we are all equal. Nothing distinguishes us from each other or makes us worthy of His presence—not race, religion, or sex; not social class, cultural status, or political power. We have no justification to think we're better than anyone else. The true freedom that Christ brings is about relationship, and it is for all of us, as is His command to love others as He loves us.

PRAY:

Lord Jesus, You have set us all on equal footing before the cross. Help me to embrace all who want to receive You as brothers and sisters, and give me Your heart's desire to make our family as big as possible.

The Problem of Evil

Read Isaiah 59:1–3, 16–21

KEY VERSES:

*The LORD's hand is not shortened, that it
cannot save; nor His ear heavy, that it cannot
hear. But your iniquities have separated you
from your God; and your sins have hidden
His face from you, so that He will not hear.*
ISAIAH 59:1–2 NKJV

UNDERSTAND:

- *How would you answer the question, "If God is
good, all-powerful, and all-knowing, why does
evil exist?"*

- *When you're facing hard times, what are your go-to
Bible verses for comfort and strength?*

APPLY:

Isaiah 59 touches on one of the biggest problems in
theology: the problem of evil. If God is good, all-powerful, and all-knowing, how can human suffering exist?
Because the level of human suffering remains as high
as it's ever been, many people respond by reasoning
that God must not be everything the Bible says He is.

The result is thinking that, while God is all-loving, He is not all-powerful (or vice-versa); He wants to help us when we're in trouble, but He can't. Isaiah 59:1 (NLT) responds to such an idea, "The LORD's arm is not too weak to save you." And to the suggestion that God isn't aware of or interested in our troubles, Isaiah 59:1 (NASB) says, "Nor is His ear so dull that it cannot hear." God permitting evil isn't the same as God producing evil. In fact, His permission must mean He has some purpose in allowing it.

Only in Jesus Christ do we have a chance of understanding that purpose. While His crucifixion was the greatest moral evil ever committed (a truly perfect, innocent man unjustly condemned), His resurrection made the greatest moral good possible: deliverance from evil for all who believe in Him.

PRAY:

Heavenly Father and Almighty God, in Jesus Christ, You have solved the problem of evil by breaking sin's hold on my heart. You have overcome the world, and Your peace and strength steady me in these wicked days.

Ready for War

Read Ephesians 6:10–18

KEY VERSE:

*A final word: Be strong in the Lord
and in his mighty power.*
EPHESIANS 6:10 NLT

UNDERSTAND:

- *What is your attitude about spiritual warfare? Who is it for? What is the nature of it?*

- *What is your tendency regarding Satan, to make too little of him or too much?*

APPLY:

Start with the biblical facts: Satan is a real, personal spirit, evil and intent on ruining your life because God loves you. Spiritual warfare is just as real as physical battle. Paul made no bones about it in Ephesians 6:10–18, clearly defining both the nature of spiritual warfare and the protection God has provided so we can fight.

Jesus blesses you because you are unified with Him. Naturally (and supernaturally), Satan attacks you at that point of unity, seeking to disrupt your connection to those blessings—the power of redemption, forgiveness, kindness, and the other fruit of the Spirit. He wants to cut you off from a full view of Jesus, and he wins when he neutralizes you through ignorance and apathy.

God has won the war against Satan, but spiritual battles continue for your growth and God's glory. When you claim the name of Christ, you enter the fray, but He has given you all you need to resist the devil and stand.

Your tour of duty will end someday, so spend your shift on alert for the enemy's movements. Like Paul in 2 Timothy 4:7 (ESV), your goal is to be able to say "I have fought the good fight, I have finished the race, I have kept the faith."

PRAY:

Lord Jesus, Almighty God, You are my commander-in-chief, the general of heaven's armies, and the victor over sin, death, and hell. I have entrusted myself to You: spirit, body, and soul. Arm me with Your power to withstand the devil's fiery darts so that I can grow to be more like You and bring glory to Your name.

About the Author

Quentin Guy writes from the high desert of New Mexico to encourage and equip people to know and serve God. His previous books include *God's Playbook for Dads* and *Prayers for Difficult Times (Men's Edition)*.